IMAGES
of America

DETROIT IN WORLD WAR I

A member of the 31st Infantry Regiment of the Michigan National guard kisses his daughter goodbye as he entrains for Camp Grayling in August 1917. This heartbreaking scene would recur thousands of times throughout the war as soldiers bid farewell to loved ones, not knowing whether their time apart would be brief or forever. (Courtesy of the Walter P. Reuther Library, Wayne State University.)

On the Cover: Belle Isle erupts in celebration as the men of the 339th Infantry, known as the "Polar Bears," disembark the SS *Britannia* and make their triumphant return home to Detroit from the Eastern Front on July 4, 1919. Thousands of residents, including these 60 "fair maidens" from the Detroit branch of the American Red Cross, turned out to shower the soldiers in flowers before a day of festivities began. (Courtesy of the Walter P. Reuther Library, Wayne State University.)

IMAGES
of America

DETROIT IN WORLD WAR I

Elizabeth Clemens

ARCADIA
PUBLISHING

ISBN 978-1-4671-1469-1

Published by Arcadia Publishing
Charleston, South Carolina

Printed in the United States of America

Library of Congress Control Number: 2015935745

For all general information, please contact Arcadia Publishing:
Telephone 843-853-2070
Fax 843-853-0044
E-mail sales@arcadiapublishing.com
For customer service and orders:
Toll-Free 1-888-313-2665

Visit us on the Internet at www.arcadiapublishing.com

In memory of Tom Featherstone

Contents

Acknowledgements		6
Introduction		7
1.	Before the War	9
2.	Draft and Recruitment	17
3.	Training and Service	37
4.	Industry	61
5.	Civilian Support	77
6.	The War's End	107

Acknowledgments

I have the good fortune of working with the staff of the Reuther Library, and I would like to thank them for their advice and support, especially Kristen Chinery. I am grateful for having met so many wonderful people in the writing of this book and would like to thank Amy Klassen of the Niagara Historical Society and Museum, Elyssa Bisoski of the Arab American National Museum, Dallas Pillen and Karen Jania from the Bentley Historical Library, and the gracious staff of the Burton Historical Collection, including Mark Bowden, Romie Minor, and Dawn Eurich. Special gratitude is extended to Arthur Wagner and Mary (Adragna) Wallace for sharing their family's story with me and Ceil Jensen of the Polish Mission of Orchard Lake. Finally, thank you to Liz Gurley and Emilia Monell of Arcadia Publishing, the loveliest people around, who made working on this project an absolute pleasure.

All uncredited photographs are from the collections of the Walter P. Reuther Library, Wayne State University, primarily the *Detroit News* Collection. The *Detroit News* Collection contains nearly 800,000 photographic negatives taken by *Detroit News* staff between the late 1800s and the mid-1980s. It was generously donated to the Reuther Library in 1997 and remains one of the most comprehensive sources in existence of Detroit's photographic history of the 20th century. Many of the reproductions used within this book were scanned directly from original 5-inch-by-7-inch glass-plate negatives, which give spectacular clarity and depth to each shot (besides being beautiful artifacts in themselves). The scenes captured by the *Detroit News* photographers are candid, emotional, and often a wonder to behold. I am impossibly grateful to these uncredited artists for the legacy they left behind.

For the sake of brevity, several abbreviations are used throughout this book to credit historical institutions who have generously shared their content:

Bentley Historical Library, University of Michigan (Bentley)
Burton Historical Collection, Detroit Public Library (Burton)
Library of Congress, Prints and Photographs Division (LOC)
National Archives and Records Administration (NARA)

Please note that all of the monetary figures in this book are the original 1917–1919 amounts and do not account for inflation.

INTRODUCTION

World War I (1914–1918) is often referred to as the first "modern war." There can be little doubt that it was the impetus that pushed Detroit firmly into the modern age. The 200 years that preceded it were a time of gentle transition from a French outpost to mercantile city and an eventual industrial center for the region. Although unknown at the time, the war would define the path Detroit was to take for the first half of the century—one of spectacular industrial, economic, and population growth. Detroit would become, within an incredibly short period, one of the largest and most influential cities in the country.

Initially, the conflict had little effect on the day-to-day activities in Detroit. Local industry benefitted from war contracts to produce materials like ambulances and cargo ships. In turn, there was an increase in the ongoing influx of new residents who came to the city seeking well-paying industrial work. As the war raged on overseas and America remained resolute in its neutrality, Detroit's immigrant communities searched for ways to support their homelands. Fundraisers were set up to provide support for endangered communities and sponsor war orphans. Surplus materials, such as clothing and food, were sent for distribution to the needy. Some men returned to Europe to fight in their native armies. Support extended to both Allied and Central Power countries because Detroit's ethnic communities were in themselves a microcosm of the European theater. Long-standing social and economic ties to Canada were sustained through material support from local organizations like the St. Andrews Society and through the voluntary enlistment of American men in the Canadian Expeditionary Forces (CAF).

The United States declared war on Germany in April 1917, and Selective Service was established just six weeks later when it became apparent that the military would not be able to find enough men to fight within their existing numbers or enlistment campaigns. This new draft was unique from those that had preceded it in that all men within the qualifying ages (21–31 years, then 18–45 years) were required to register, and it took men from across all social and economic classes. Men with particular talents, such as medical professionals, engineers, and mechanics, were heavily recruited into the American Expeditionary Forces (AEF). Detroit gave nearly 23,000 men during the first year of the draft; an equal amount joined the military voluntarily. As one might imagine, the situation weighed heavily on the hearts of many citizens who had to learn to adjust to life without their sons, husbands, and brothers.

Turning the motley group of "selects" into a fighting force was a difficult prospect for the officers of the AEF. The men came from many backgrounds in terms of skills and education. Most of the Detroit selects were initially sent to the newly built Camp Custer in Battle Creek, Michigan. The mobilized National Guard and their new recruits (31st, 32nd, and 33rd Infantry Brigades) were sent to Camp Grayling to train, eventually moving to Camp MacArthur in Waco, Texas. Selfridge Field was established in Mount Clemens as a training center for aviation. Mobilization proved faster than production capabilities, and it took months for the men to be fully equipped with the necessary supplies. Most troops were not ready to leave for Europe until the winter of

1917–1918, but they had plenty to do in the meantime. Representatives from European armies were sent to the camps to prepare the men for the "modern" style of warfare that had been raging in Europe for the past three years, which included using technological advancements in weaponry, chemical and bunker warfare, and the use of tanks, airplanes, and submarines on a wide scale, something American troops had little experience with. These advancements in warfare resulted in a huge human cost: approximately 10 million men died on the battlefields of Europe and the Near East during the conflict. Of the 175,000 troops that Michigan sent to war, 5,000 perished from combat injuries or disease.

By the time the United States joined the fray, the Allied and Central Powers had decimated each other's forces to the point that the war had transformed into a "war of production," one in which the advantage belonged to the side with the best industrial output rather than skills of troops or military leaders. In this environment, Detroit was in the perfect position to flex its new industrial muscle. Techniques for mass production were already tested and in place thanks to the ongoing evolution of the automobile industry. The city was filled with innovative minds eager to find ways to push the production limit and engineers ready to turn these ideas into reality. Detroit was the recipient of vast amounts of government contracts, and its many factories were quickly retooled to produce munitions, tanks, plating for armored cars, submarine chasers, airplanes, ambulances, field kitchens, and just about everything else under the sun. The development of Liberty Engines, headed by Detroit engineers and produced in its factories, proved instrumental in the success of the Allied forces.

The effects of the draft were keenly felt in Detroit, where its war industry lost workers faster than they could recruit them. The city faced a surplus of work without the manpower to fulfill contracts or run day-to-day operations. In response, women were recruited to work in areas that were formerly off-limits to them, such as the war industry, public and transportation services, and the military. These advancements in the industrial workforce, though mostly temporary, would pave the way for the introduction of women's suffrage and change the way the public viewed the role of women in modern society.

Whether it was ties to the old country, a loved one in the service, or simply a sense of duty, Detroit's citizens mobilized into a powerhouse to support the war effort. Detroit was continually at the top of the national lists for charitable giving, be it through government-sponsored Liberty Loans or Red Cross campaigns. The legacy of giving is remarkable considering many of its people had very little resources to share. In addition to fundraising, citizens contributed in smaller, personal ways, such as participating in food conservation, rolling bandages, and sewing and knitting gear for the troops. Volunteerism was nearly universal, with the Red Cross dominating the scene. Thousands of women joined the Detroit Red Cross and took on a wide variety of tasks, including feeding visiting soldiers, training women as nurses to serve locally (where there was a shortage of medical professionals) and overseas, and providing services for the families of the military. During the influenza epidemics, volunteers were particularly important, aiding victims of the sickness at great risk to their own health.

In the end, the home front proved equally as important as the soldier fighting on the western front in the outcome of the war. The civilian population raised the money the government needed to finance the war, provided the manpower to fuel the war industry, conserved food and supplies to support the troops, and saw to the needs of soldiers at home and abroad through volunteerism. Armistice was declared on November 11, 1918, and over the next nine months, troops would slowly come home. Local pride in the accomplishments of its men would color Detroit's social activities for years to come.

By war's end, Detroit was the fifth-largest city in America and a center for innovation in a number of different fields, including industry and aviation. Many long-standing views on gender and class had been challenged by wartime accomplishments. Detroit—ever resilient, clever, and industrious—had charmed the world with its "can do" attitude and proved itself to be one of the great cities of the modern age.

One

Before the War

When the first shot of war rang out on August 22, 1914, Detroit was in a transitional period of physical, industrial, economic, and population growth. Though the war seemed very much a world away, its influence would challenge the way the city viewed issues of industrialization, urbanization, and the struggle for equality between social classes, gender, and race.

At the dawn on the 20th century, Detroit was one of the fastest growing cities in America. Outside of New York and Chicago, it was the most popular destination for incoming immigrants. In addition, thousands of families moved to Detroit from the rural South. Between 1910 and 1920, Detroit's population nearly doubled, going from 456,766 to 993,678. Here, an immigrant arrives in the city, likely at the newly constructed Michigan Central Station, around 1913.

Many people were drawn to Detroit by the promise of work and a fair wage in the city's many factories. The development of the assembly line facilitated tremendous industrial growth and employment opportunity. Detroit's industrial expertise and innovation would prove vital to the war effort in the years to come. Shown here are workers on the magneto assembly line in Ford Motor Company's Highland Park plant in 1913.

Few events shaped the history of the city like the Great Migration. Between 1915 and 1930, thousands of African Americans were drawn to Detroit to escape the economic collapse in the South and find industrial work. They found a slightly better social situation but faced challenges nonetheless, including de-facto segregation in many areas of their lives. Here, men enjoy a ball game viewed from the segregated section of Navin Field.

Detroit's immigrant community was diverse to say the least. Nationalities spanned the globe, from the Northern reaches of Europe to the eastern shores of China. The "Americanization" movement took hold during this time as an answer to problems that arose due to language barriers and differences in social custom. Immigrants were taught elementary English, civics, and American ideals of hygiene and housekeeping in classes sponsored by industries, community organizations, or the city.

Germans first arrived in Detroit in the 1830s. By the 1880s, twenty percent of the city's population was German-born. The community was a mixture of professionals, teachers, musicians, and laborers. Germantown, the area between the Jefferson and Gratiot corridors on the lower East Side, was the community's center. Seen here is Harmonie Hall, located at the corner of Lafayette and Beaubien Streets. The building was a neighborhood meeting space and home to the Harmonie Society, Detroit's oldest musical association.

During the early war years, Detroit's German community was generally viewed as well assimilated, though some citizens doubted their loyalty. Everything changed in June 1915 when a series of bombs rocked southern Ontario, targeting buildings related to the Allied war effort. Seen here at center is the ringleader of the plot, Albert Kaltschmidt. Kaltschmidt was a German native living in Detroit who had the monetary assistance of Count von Bernstorff, the German ambassador to the United States.

The Kaltschmidt case proved that fears of disloyalty within the German community were not entirely unfounded. Once the United States entered the war, Germans were labeled "enemy aliens" and forced to register with the government or face internment. Many German Americans turned away from their heritage in an attempt to be more "American." Traditional costumes, like those seen here, would stay out of sight until well after the war came to a close.

As conditions deteriorated overseas, Detroit's ethnic communities looked homeward, desperate to help. Members of Detroit's Greek, Syrian, and Armenian communities were active with the American Committee for Relief in the Near East. The organization is credited with saving approximately one million lives during the humanitarian crisis caused by the dissolution of the Ottoman Empire. It provided food, medical care, and established centers to care for children orphaned during the Armenian genocide.

During the war, Detroit was home to one of the largest Belgian communities in the United States. In August 1915, Father Syoens, pastor of Our Lady of Sorrows Church, went to Eastern Flanders on a mission of mercy and brought back 116 Belgian war orphans. The children, seen here at the immigration station, were placed with family members already established in Detroit or were taken in by foster families.

A food shortage early in the war forced Belgium into near starvation conditions. In response, the Commission for Relief in Belgium was formed to supply food and other relief to areas of Belgium and northern France under German occupation. The cause was held dear by many Detroiters, who actively raised funds and conserved food for the effort. Belgian children are shown here dining on food sent to Europe through the Belgian Relief Fund. (LOC.)

While some worked to alleviate the suffering of those affected by war, others tried to put a stop to the conflict altogether. In December 1915, Henry Ford sponsored an expedition to Europe with 150 other prominent activists. The mission, dubbed as the "Peace Ship," sought to bring pacifists from other non-combatant countries together to broker a lasting peace. Plagued by infighting, influenza, and lack of support by warring nations, the mission was ultimately a failure.

Foreign military, including the Serbian, Greek, and Italian armies, came to Detroit to persuade immigrant men to return home to fight. Sicilian-born Salvatore "Sam" Adragna was one of thousands of men who answered the call. Adragna fought in the Balkans as part of the Italian Cavalry. His war experience was one of intense situations and extreme deprivation. After the war, Adragna married his sweetheart, Anna, and settled permanently on Detroit's East Side. (Adragna family.)

As a border city with long-standing social ties to Canada and with a significant population that was of Canadian or British descent, Detroit was an excellent recruiting site for the Canadian Expeditionary Force (CEF). Although exact numbers are scarce, it is known that significant numbers of Detroit men enlisted in local battalions such as the 99th, the Kent Scottish, and the 241st Essex, who logged 27 percent of new recruits as Americans at one recruitment drive in 1916. Men risked more than their lives by volunteering with the CEF. Native-born Americans who crossed the border to fight with Commonwealth forces risked a loss of citizenship upon their return. At left is a recruiting poster for the British-Canadian recruiting mission. Below, recruits of the Essex Fusiliers march through Windsor, Ontario, around 1917 or 1918. (At left, Herbert Hoover Presidential Library.)

Two

DRAFT AND RECRUITMENT

The United States formally entered World War I on April 6, 1917. The sudden passage of the Selective Service Act just six weeks later was a shock to many people. Unlike the drafts of previous wars, one could not buy a deferral. All men between the ages of 21 and 31, from lumber baron to day laborer, had an equal chance for selection. Here, a soldier receives an affectionate goodbye as he departs for training camp.

There were three draft registrations during World War I. The first, held on June 5, 1917, was for all men between the ages of 21 and 31. The second, on June 5, 1918, registered those who attained age 21 in the year prior. The third registration was held on September 12, 1918, and included men between 18 and 45. Though some animals, like horses, could be drafted into service, it appears this dog was in line purely for moral support.

On June 5, 1917, an incredible 154,700 of Detroit's men registered for the draft. Booths opened throughout the city at 7:00 a.m., and the wait lasted for hours depending on one's district. A lottery was drawn on July 20, 1917, to select the men who would serve based on quotas calculated from a city's population of draft-eligible men. Within this quota system, Detroit was required to send approximately 22,000 men into military service during the first year of war.

Registration was slow in districts with large foreign-born populations, and some booths worked through the night until the following dawn. The delay was caused by the fact that many of their residents were male industrial workers of draft-age. The language barrier further slowed the paperwork process. Police were on hand to help sort out bad tempers caused by the long wait or animosity between rival ethnic groups.

The Second District of the Third Ward had the widest variety of ethnic groups reporting. African Americans, Hungarians, Italians, Greeks, Serbs, Croats, Bosnians, Finns, Bulgarians, Romanians, Turks, Chinese, Swedes, Germans, Austrians, and Canadians all lived in the district, located near St. Antoine on Detroit's Lower East Side. A separate registration was held for many of Detroit's Chinese residents due to difficulties in translating birth dates from the Chinese calendar system.

Draft exemptions were given for a number of circumstances, including medical conditions, immigration status, criminal history, and religious vocation. Men with dependent families, or workers in essential industry, were considered, though the reprieve was often only temporary. Nearly 54,700 men requested exemption in Detroit's first draft; the majority were denied. Here, a line of men seen fit to serve leaves for training camp.

Rules were amended early in the draft process to allow for alien selects to waive their exemption and fight in the US Army. In return, they were typically awarded US citizenship upon their discharge. Such was the case of Sam Hussein Unis, who was only in the country for four months before he was drafted willingly into service. Unis is seen here (center) posing with friends while encamped at Fort Sheridan in 1918. (Arab American Museum.)

Examining boards were set up in public buildings throughout the city to ensure men were of sufficient physical health for combat. Potential soldiers needed to be between 5 feet and 6 feet, 8 inches tall, with weight proportional to their height, have good vision and hearing, and be free of disease. Chest measurements were an important indicator of health, as were "flat feet"—both were thought to be indicators of hidden disease, such as tuberculosis.

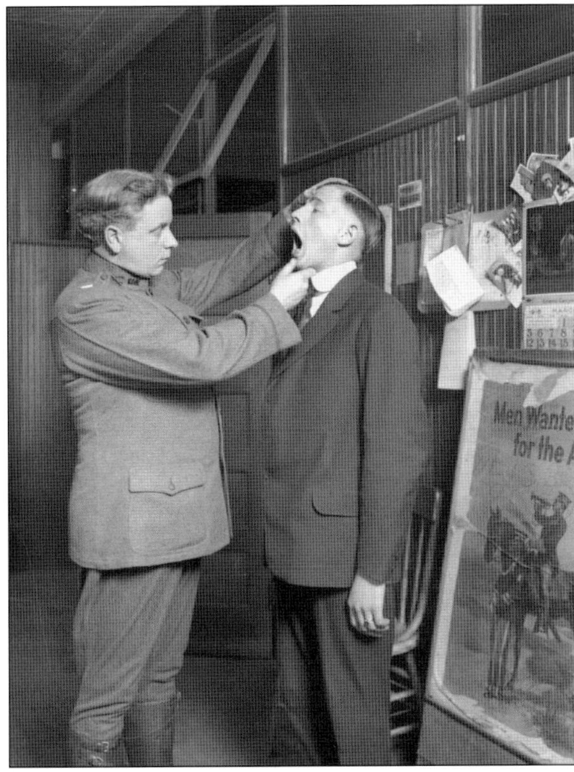

It seemed that the entire city turned out to watch the first group of draftees leave for camp in the summer of 1917. The streets surrounding Campus Martius were filled to capacity, and people took to higher vantage points, such as trees, statues, windows, and rooftops, to get a good view of the spectacle.

A procession was held as draftees made their way to the train station to lend a patriotic flavor to the day. Bands, local personalities, and banners guided the men through narrow breaks in the massive crowd. In this photograph, women and men in costume carry flags of the Allied nations during the draft parade.

The draft parade featured local social, industrial, and political leaders. Henry Ford (center) marches with Detroit mayor Oscar Marx (at right) through the crowds at Campus Martius. Though Ford was a pacifist, he supported the war after America entered the conflict by selling products at a discount to the government, investing heavily in Liberty Bonds, and creating jobs in his plants that accommodated veterans disabled during the war.

Emotions ran high as friends and family members said goodbye to the conscripted men. City officials feared that violent outbursts by angry citizens or anti-draft organizations were a distinct possibility. In response to this, hundreds of police officers patrolled the event, on foot and on horseback, to make sure the departure of the drafted men was without contest or incident.

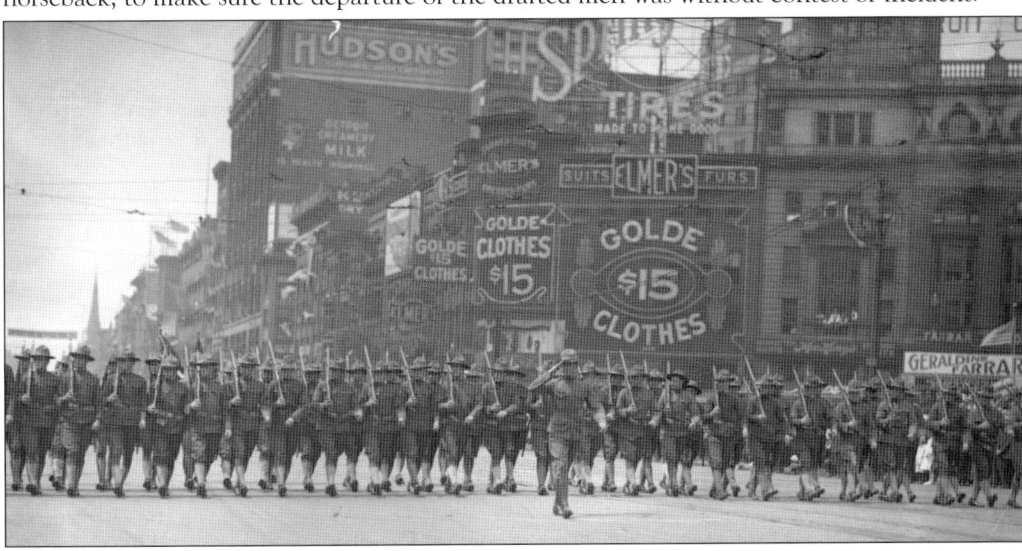

The 31st Infantry Regiment of the Michigan National Guard is one of the oldest military organizations in the United States. During the Great War, it was the first Detroit outfit to leave the city and see service overseas. The idea of serving with friends, family members, and fellow Detroiters was a comforting thought to many men of draft age, thus the 31st was a popular regiment amongst recruits.

Detroiters loved the 31st Infantry. The week prior to their departure saw one celebratory event after another. When it came time to bid them farewell, however, the mood turned somber, and crowds were relatively small and silent. Families and friends, well versed by the daily papers in the horrors that awaited the soldiers overseas, bid tearful farewells as their loved ones entrained for Camp Grayling.

Enlistment numbers for the first year were 22,720, slightly outpacing drafted men at 22,280. Patriotism drew many, as well as the desire to choose what branch of the military they would serve in instead of leaving it up to the draft board. Many volunteers were eager for adventure and a chance to define themselves in a meaningful way. Here, excited recruits leave Detroit for training camp in 1917.

Draftees and recruits left the city in large waves, usually preceded by a parade from the armory or wherever they were to muster, to Michigan Central Station. The events were typically well attended and celebratory in nature with musical accompaniment from regimental bands. It was not unusual for friends and family members to leave their decorum at the curb and march alongside the soldiers, as seen here.

A soldier leaving for training at Camp Custer receives assistance from a friend as he leans out of a railcar at Michigan Central Station to say goodbye to a young woman, most likely his fiancée or wife. It became impossible for romantic scenes like this to continue as more and more men were drafted into service and the volume of people on the platform developed into a safety and security concern.

This scene played out over and over throughout a three-day deployment of 5,000 conscripted men in November 1917. Mothers, wives, fathers, and sweethearts lined the gates along the back of the station on Fifteenth Avenue, waiting patiently for hours to catch one last glimpse of their loved one. The deployment was scheduled to leave in October but was delayed because training camps were still under construction.

Because of its proximity to Michigan Central Station, Navin Field (later known as Tiger Stadium) was often used as a staging ground for recruits and troops leaving the city. Parades and bands were often employed to lend a sense of pageantry to situations that could prove emotionally taxing for the citizenry. Here, draft selects from the West Side Local Board No. 25 march across the playing field toward Michigan Central Station.

A group of African American draftees and recruits, part of the great "Second Draft" of June 1918, walks through Navin Field preparing to leave for military training. Though the men were deemed fit to serve in the military by draft board officials, they were sent to training on separate days from their white counterparts and were immediately segregated upon their arrival at Camp Custer.

Heartbroken friends and family members watched from the streets leading up to Michigan Central Station as their loved ones departed for camp. By this point in the war, American troops were fighting in France. Horrific casualty lists, reports of battles in the papers, or stories delivered by word of mouth drove fear into the hearts of people who had soldiers entering military service.

Detroit was home to a number of groups that protested American involvement in the war, including pacifists, socialists, and radical labor organizations, such as the Industrial Workers of the World (IWW). The IWW was firm in its belief that the war was a concern for capitalists, not the workers. Its refusal to call a halt to strikes in war industries and encouragement of draft evasion resulted in many members being tried under the Espionage Act. Bill Haywood, leader of the IWW, poses for a photograph (third from the right) outside of the Wage Workers Book Shop, located at 278 Gratiot Avenue, around 1919 or 1920.

Hundreds of men were arrested on suspicion of anti-draft or anti-war activities. Maurice Sugar, at right with his wife, Jane, was one such activist. The labor lawyer was indicted, convicted, and sentenced to a year in prison in the summer of 1917 for refusing to register for the draft. He was disbarred from practicing law until 1923, when he obtained a pardon from Judge Frank Murphy. A written account of his stay at the Detroit House of Corrections, *300 Days*, is available for research at the Walter P. Reuther Library. Below is a view of the Detroit House of Corrections, where Sugar and hundreds of other anti-war activists and political dissidents were held.

The Navy was promoted as an adventurous means to complete military service. For many, "adventure" on the high seas (or local waterways) was far preferable to life in the trenches. Recruitment figures for the first year of the war testify to this fact, as the Navy was only slightly behind the Army in total enlistment numbers. Young Naval volunteers wearing and carrying recruitment banners gather together in downtown Detroit (above) and bid farewell to friends and family (below) as they prepare to depart for training. The men would most likely serve locally, at the Naval Training Center at River Rouge, or at the Great Lakes Naval Academy in Illinois.

Legendary bandmaster John Philip Sousa spent a week in Detroit during November 1917 with his 300-piece Great Lakes Naval Training Station Band. The group made numerous appearances throughout the city at parades, concerts, and balls to aid in the recruitment of Naval trainees and to help in fundraising efforts. Above, Sousa leads his band during one of many public displays. Below, the Great Lakes Naval Training Band and famed soprano Anna Case sing the "Star-Spangled Banner" during a downtown concert given before an appreciative crowd.

As part of the November 1917 recruitment festivities, Detroit got a visit from SC-173, a newly launched submarine chaser. The petite, yet heavily armed wooden ship was a hit with the crowds and undoubtedly lured a few men to the enlistment office. Three of her sixteen crew members were Detroit natives and are seen here standing on the deck. They are, from left to right, C.A Riopelle, seaman first class; E.J. Bois, cook; and M.L. Sinnett, seaman first class.

Pres. Theodore Roosevelt made one of his last visits to Detroit on May 30, 1918, at the request of Ens. D.J.D. Coleman, head of naval recruitment in Detroit. The popular president was brought to Detroit in an effort to aid in recruitment for the Navy. Roosevelt shares a laugh with Coleman while flanked by adoring Detroit "Jackies" (naval sailors) and members of the river patrol outside of the Detroit Athletic Club.

Edward Denby, president of the Detroit Chamber of Commerce, is seen here with Mayor Marx as he presents the colors to Naval Reserves in Cadillac Square. Later in the year, the former congressman would enlist as a private in the United States Marine Corps, achieving the rank of major by the time he was discharged in 1919. Denby would finish out his military career as secretary of the Navy, an appointment given to him by President Harding in 1921.

Detroit's Naval Reservists were called to war in August 1918 to man newly built ships and replace civilians aboard the transport ships that carried troops and supplies. Their clerical and administrative duties were mostly reassigned to newly enlisted women. Reservists, followed by a thick crowd of family and friends, march down Randolph Street as they prepare to leave Detroit for active service.

August 18, 1918, was lauded as "Navy Day" in Detroit. In celebration, an "attack" on Belle Isle was planned. Sailors, disguised as Germans, formed landing parties and snuck across the Detroit River in cutters. They were met by a barrage of blank cartridges fired from Michigan State troops entrenched within the Athletic Field. An enthusiastic crowd, estimated at 100,000, was in attendance on the island and along the shore of the river.

Civilian craft were also drafted into service. John F. Dodge's yacht *NOKOMIS*, and eventually her sister *NOKOMIS II*, were requisitioned by the Navy, outfitted for duty, and used to patrol the Eastern Seaboard. This is a view of the farewell party for *NOKOMIS* as she is handed over to the Navy. From left to right are John F. Dodge, Adolph Vocell, Albert A. Andrich, an unidentified Navy official, Robert Jackson, Edward T. Fitzgerald, Horace E. Dodge, and Mayor Oscar Marx.

Recruitment for foreign armies continued after the United States entered the war. On October 19 and 20, 1917, members of the famed Canadian Black Watch visited Detroit during a British-Canadian military recruitment campaign. The men, a mixture of seasoned veterans and new recruits, visited numerous factories, marched in several parades, hosted a concert at Grand Circus Park, and shared war stories with the public at a mass meeting held at the armory.

Members of a "Jewish Battalion" pose for a photograph before leaving in April 1918 for World War I. The young men were recruits of the Jewish Legion, which actively recruited in Detroit. Established by the British government in 1917, the legion was comprised of approximately 5,000 soldiers from North America and the British Empire. The Detroit contingent, seen here, trained in Canada before making its way to Palestine to help liberate the region from Turkish rule.

The liberation of Poland weighed heavy on the minds of Detroit's Polish community. Approximately 3,000 Detroit soldiers traveled to Niagara-on-the-Lake, Ontario, to train for military service in a volunteer-based Polish army. The force, sponsored by France, became known as "Haller's Army," after its leader, Gen. Jozef Haller. The men fought fiercely throughout France and were deployed to Poland postwar to stop the Bolshevik advance. Ignancy Jan Paderewski addresses Haller's Army at Camp Niagara. (Niagara Historical Society.)

Each of the soldiers in this photograph had their own story to tell. Hipolit Wagner kneels third from left. Born in Idalin, Lublin Province, Poland, Wagner immigrated to Detroit in 1913. He received his paramilitary training through the Polish Falcons and was inducted into Haller's Army in 1918. Wagner was an eloquent diarist, and his experiences were later published as a memoir called *My Journey in the World.* (Arthur Wagner family.)

Three

TRAINING AND SERVICE

Officers had their work cut out for them in turning the rookies into a fighting force. The volunteers and draftees had been many things in their past life—laborers, tailors, musicians, clerks—but few were familiar with soldiering. Men at Camp Custer are seen here learning to march. Many are without uniforms because the war moved at a faster pace than production.

Fluid construction plans, a shortage of skilled construction workers, and bad weather played large roles in the delay of the completion of Camp Custer. The camp, located near Battle Creek, was formally handed over to the government on November 15, 1917, several months after troops started training there. Despite the setbacks, the community, complete with hundreds of buildings and able to house 40,000 men, was raised from corn fields in a little over four months.

Soldiers were directed to the intake booths immediately upon arrival to Camp Custer. Their barn-like appearance probably resonated with the men as they were herded through by the hundreds. Men were divided up by local board number to be checked in. Officers are pictured waiting inside the receiving station to check in the next trainload of recruits and draftees.

Living arrangements lacked many of the domestic comforts of home, a fact amplified by large amounts of men living in close quarters. Over 100,000 men moved through Camp Custer during the war, each leaving their own mark on the camp. A sunny day has prompted members of the 339th Infantry to give their mattresses an airing from barrack windows.

In response to the dramatic changes in warfare since the United States last engaged in a major conflict, officers from European allies were brought to US training camps to help prepare soldiers for the current practices of modern warfare. Here, a soldier at Camp Custer takes instruction from a French officer, likely Capt. Robert Laussel of the French Army, on how to use a machine gun on October 17, 1917. (Bentley.)

Machine guns became a defining characteristic of World War I. The powerful weapons required extensive training to learn how to group shots, handle recoil, take aim, and manage jams. Infantrymen practice handling guns at an unidentified location, likely Camp Custer, around 1917.

Although not nearly as complex to work with as the machine gun, equally as mysterious to the uninitiated was the rifle. City dwellers would have had little use for such weaponry in their civilian lives, and the experience of cleaning, assembling, and learning to accurately fire a rifle posed a challenge for many during the early days of training. Seen here around 1917, soldiers take aim at the Camp Grayling rifle range.

For many soldiers, bayonet instruction and drills were their first real exposure to the violence that was expected of them. The men practiced thrusting movements for half-hour blocks at a time until they learned how to effectively "clear" their weapon from their sandbag victim. Here, men from the 338th Division aim for vital organs during a bayonet-fighting class at Camp Custer.

Wooden artillery, jokingly nicknamed "the pride of the 320th," had to suffice until the real weaponry arrived at Camp Custer. For four weeks, artillery regiments studied the various pieces of the wooden counterparts and practiced servicing and moving them, as pictured. Four 3-inch field pieces were delivered to the camp in November 1917, much to the delight of the soldiers.

Few exercises were as dreaded as anti-gas training. The men were trained to sense gas attacks and get masks on within six seconds through a series of drills: first, unprotected exposure to Lachrymose gas in a gas house; then exposure, with equipment on hand, in a trench. Those unfortunates who failed the trench test by not recognizing the gas or getting their mask on in time became test patients for medical staff.

The use of cavalry troops against enemy infantry came to an end during the war when it became apparent that the horses were not suited to compete with the elements of modern warfare, such as machine guns, barbed wire, and trenches. Nevertheless, the military continued to incorporate cavalry into training. Soldiers are seen running through a practice cavalry charge during maneuvers, most likely at Camp Grayling.

As part of their training, men were taught to hand-dig and fight within trench systems. At Camp Custer, the men built a half-mile long front used for training exercises. It featured two complete sets of fire trenches, support, reserve, communication trenches, machine-gun encampments, warrens of dugouts, climbing posts, and listening posts. A barbed-wired no-man's-land separated the two systems. In this image, the 160th Artillery Brigade works on gun pit construction in October 1917.

Trench warfare created a host of new challenges, both from a logistical and medical standpoint. One of the most common side effects of life in the trenches was "trench foot." The infection is brought on by standing in damp environments for long periods of time and can develop into gangrene when left untreated. Soldiers at Camp Custer are pictured learning how to inspect their feet for signs of infection.

It was imperative for military officers to have an advanced understanding of the French language before their deployment overseas. To help with this need, the YMCA set up and ran schools in many of the training camps throughout the country. Officers of the 339th Infantry, stationed at Camp Custer, are listening to a phonograph during a French lesson in 1917. (Bentley.)

The YMCA also ran schools to help immigrant soldiers learn to speak and read English. Camp Custer was one of the first Army camps to teach foreign-born students English in "the dramatic method," a way of teaching that illustrates every idea by action. Once the soldier proved conversant, he was given a course in civics. Members of the 329th Field Artillery are seen participating in an elementary English class in October 1917. (Bentley.)

Over 2,000 African American soldiers came to Camp Custer during the war. From the very start, segregation proved to be a problem for soldiers and camp planners. When the first two African American soldiers arrived at camp in November 1917, their barracks were not yet complete, so they were placed in tents at the edge of camp. Language classes were held separately and were crowded—one French class had 130 pupils. Because the soldiers could not use the social hall to entertain guests, another space had to be secured. The War Camp Community Service found an unused factory room, which it cleaned, decorated, and equipped. Above, soldiers entertain visiting family and friends at their social club. Below is a view of crowded, segregated classrooms. (Bentley.)

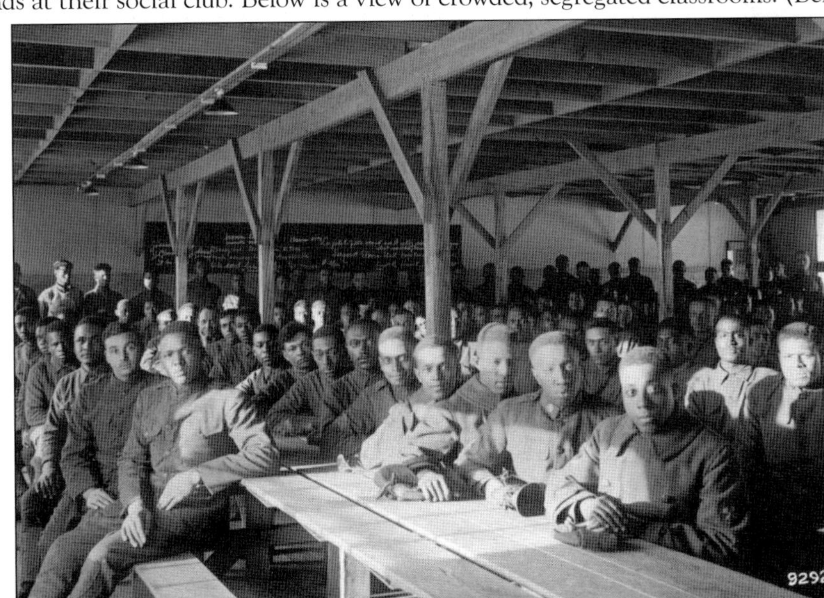

The American Library Association (ALA) provided wartime services to enlisted men at home and abroad. They set up and maintained staffed libraries in military hospitals, built libraries in 36 army camps, and provided small book collections for seamen on merchant ships. In Detroit, ALA book drives and fundraising were done through the Detroit Public Library. This is the interior of the ALA-sponsored library at Camp Custer in 1917. (University of Illinois Archives.)

There were many opportunities for recreation besides the library at Camp Custer. The soldiers had their own baseball teams, a theatre where they could stage plays, a social hall for general tomfoolery, and their own camp band. The band had nearly 100 members, the majority of whom were musicians drafted into service out of Detroit. Besides providing the camp with entertainment, the band toured throughout the state to play concerts at public venues. (LOC.)

Mass in the field was a very different experience for soldiers accustomed to praying in one of Detroit's beautiful, historic churches, but the basic elements were the same. A priest wearing vestments delivers outdoor Mass, likely at Camp Grayling. The liturgy is accompanied by the camp band, seen at left. At right, a makeshift altar is covered in the American flag, and in the distance a processional cross is in view.

For many new soldiers, the trip to training camp was their first lengthy experience away from home; others had never even been outside of the city. Letters and packages were vital to morale, both in the camps and with the families left behind. These men take a moment in the YMCA recreation hut to write a note home.

The Military Draft Act of 1917 prohibited certain items, such as alcohol, or actions, such as prostitution, within or near military camps. Visitors, volunteers, and enlisted men entering and exiting camps were subject to inspection to ensure compliance. A guard looks through the luggage of two men at Camp Custer in search of alcoholic beverages. (Bentley.)

Members of the Michigan National Guard's 31st Infantry Regiment, having returned to Detroit after service along the Mexican border in Texas, arrive at the gates of Detroit's Fort Wayne. Built in 1842 to defend the United States against potential British incursion from Canada, the fort has never weathered a single shot. It has, however, served as induction station for Michigan troops entering into armed conflicts, from the Civil War to the Vietnam War.

During World War I, Fort Wayne hosted a number of different military units, including approximately 1,300 segregated African American troops, seen here, who were relegated to construction work. It also served as an acquisition center for military motor vehicles and parts manufactured in Detroit. This role would be further developed in World War II, when Fort Wayne would become the largest military motor-supply depot in the world.

Camp Grayling, located outside of Grayling, Michigan, was founded in 1913 as the designated mobilization center for Michigan National Guard Troops. During World War I, it housed and trained the 31st and 32nd Infantry Regiments. The difference between the facilities at Camp Custer and Camp Grayling are rather startling. Though Camp Grayling had far less in terms of facilities, the splendid forest environment more than made up for it. The soldiers pictured here take lessons on a hillside as others drill in the distance.

The open-air training of Camp Grayling was not suited to Michigan winters, thus the men of the 32nd Infantry Regiment, shown here, were sent to southern training grounds at Camp MacArthur, just outside of Waco, Texas. Along with National Guard troops from Wisconsin, they would form the 32nd Infantry Division. The division arrived in France in February and quickly earned the nickname "Les Terribles" for their fierce fighting style and impressive battle record.

The 85th Infantry Division (known as the "Custer Division") was made up of soldiers primarily from Michigan and included the 337th, 338th, 339th, and 340th Infantry Regiments. It was activated on August 25, 1917, at Camp Custer and trained for nearly a year. The division was split between fronts upon their arrival in England. The 339th famously fought in northern Russia, while the others fought throughout France. This image was taken when the 85th Division stopped in Detroit en route to Europe.

In August 1918, a re-staging of the famed Battle of Vimy Ridge was given at the state fairgrounds in Detroit. Performing with airplanes on loan from Selfridge Field, tanks furnished by the Rouge plant, and live mortars, mines, and field artillery were 2,000 members of the 551st Brigade of the Michigan State Troops. The proceeds raised went to repair the armory and to provide heavy winter clothing to National Guardsmen.

The highlight of the event came at dusk, when a canvas "mimic city," complete with its own twin-tower cathedral and town square, burst into flames and crumbled to ruin. The showcase, witnessed by 15,000 awed spectators, was orchestrated through the help of Maj. J.F. Templeton, a Canadian Expeditionary Forces veteran of Vimy Ridge, who provided the men with an exact copy of the military orders from the battle. The "Germans" pictured here gamely surrender to the "Canadians."

The Home Guard was a volunteer outfit that provided cities with protection during the war in the absence of the National Guard. In Detroit, the men were stationed at docks and stockyards and patrolled areas of importance to the war effort. Here, Detroit's Home Guard marches in a parade along Woodward Avenue in 1918.

The military saw sports figures, both professional players and local university heroes, as valuable training tools. Due to their athletic prowess, the men adapted easily to training and were often seen as candidates for elevated positions because their fellow soldiers admired and respected them. Corp. Richard "Red" Shields of the Detroit Heralds football team works the wooden artillery gun at Camp Custer in the fall of 1917.

Unpatriotic as it may seem, thousands of Tigers fans let out a collective moan when it was announced that Ty Cobb had enlisted and was commissioned as a captain in the US Army. Cobb reported for duty on October 1, 1918, as part of the Chemical Warfare Service. After a brief training period, he was on his way overseas. Many of his teammates served the Allied effort by spending the extended offseason in Detroit's war plants. Oscar Stanage served as an airplane inspector at Lincoln Motors Company, Ed Killian worked on shells, Bobby Vech and Archie Yelle made 450-pound, 10-inch shells at the American Car & Foundry Company, Nemo Liebold built airplane wings at Fisher Body, and Harry Covelskie built Liberty engines. (LOC.)

Detroit race car driver Eddie Rickenbacker started the war as General Pershing's personal chauffeur and ended it as a world-famous flying ace. Rickenbacker was fascinated by planes and was certain his training as a racer would translate well to the skies. After leaving Pershing and working as an engineering officer, Rickenbacker convinced his superiors to let him join the 94th Aero Squadron. Between April 29 and October 30, 1918, he shot down 26 enemy planes, setting the American record for the war. The flying ace ended the war as a captain and commander of his squadron. Rickenbacker returned to Detroit after the war to start Rickenbacker Motor Company and remained an important figure in Detroit's postwar aviation circles.

Detroit's waterways were patrolled by a fleet of craft made up of both military and appropriated civilian ships. The grand lady of them all was the USS *Wolverine*, launched in 1843 as the first iron-hulled warship in the Navy. Her crew of 130 sailors never encountered a U-Boat, but the *Wolverine* and other ships witnessed rumrunners, illegal water crossings, drifting fisherman, and other lively goings-on along the Canadian border.

The Michigan Naval Militia trained aboard the USS *Don Juan D'Austria* during the first months of the war. The ship was launched on January 23, 1887, as part of the Spanish fleet. She was captured by the United States and commissioned as a training vessel in 1900. The *Don Juan D'Austria* was recommissioned in the summer of 1917 and served as a patrol boat and escort ship throughout the Eastern Seaboard for the duration of the war.

The government was keen on making Detroit a center of aeronautics during the war, so it only made sense that an aviation-training base would be established in the area. Work began on Selfridge Field in early June, and it took 1,600–2,000 men six weeks to level the former marshland and construct over 50 buildings. It was named for Lt. Thomas Selfridge, the first US aviator to die in an air accident. Occupancy was established in August 1917, with room to train 900 aviators. The pilots were very expensive to train—an estimated cost of $75,000 each—due to the fact that they were likely to damage one or two planes during training. Above is a composite print of the construction of Selfridge and the men responsible for it, including Harry Hutton, Ray D. Chapin, Eugene Lewis, Howard E. Coffin, and Henry B. Joy. Below, Selfridge planes are seen at the ready.

Selfridge had a number of different schools that trained men in specific areas of aviation. Besides training fliers, it had a school that trained airplane and gasoline engine mechanics, as well as an aerial gunnery school. The aerial gunnery school was lauded by the Department of War to be one of the best schools of its kind in the United States or abroad. The training grounds included eight miles of targets over Lake St. Clair and the surrounding land. Above, machine-gunner trainees practice shooting at targets in Lake St. Clair. Below, members of the 8th Aero Squadron pose for a group photograph while on duty in France. The squadron was brought to Selfridge in July 1917 and, along with the 9th Aero Squadron, helped build the flying field. The 8th Aero trained at Selfridge for three and a half months before taking leave for Europe. (NARA.)

Boxing exercises, like those seen in this image taken at Selfridge Field, were not just for sport and amusement. Despite being seen as a "low" sort of sport at the time, boxing was promoted in training camps because it required strength and endurance and taught a soldier to anticipate his opponent's movement and protect himself—important skills when fighting hand to hand or with bayonets.

The sheer volume of casualties on the western front made the mobilization of medical units a priority. The enlisted staff of Harper Hospital mobilized almost immediately after the United States' declaration of war. Unfortunately, enthusiasm and efficiency could not overcome supply shortages. The unit would not make it to France until summer. Shown here is a view of the flag presentation ceremony for Base Hospital No. 17, the new home of the Harper unit.

These Harper Hospital nurses, en route to France, take in some fresh air and pose for a snapshot aboard the SS *Mongolia*. The ship, launched on the auspicious day of Friday, August 13, 1917, was chased by a submarine through the danger zone just off the North American coast but made it to France unharmed.

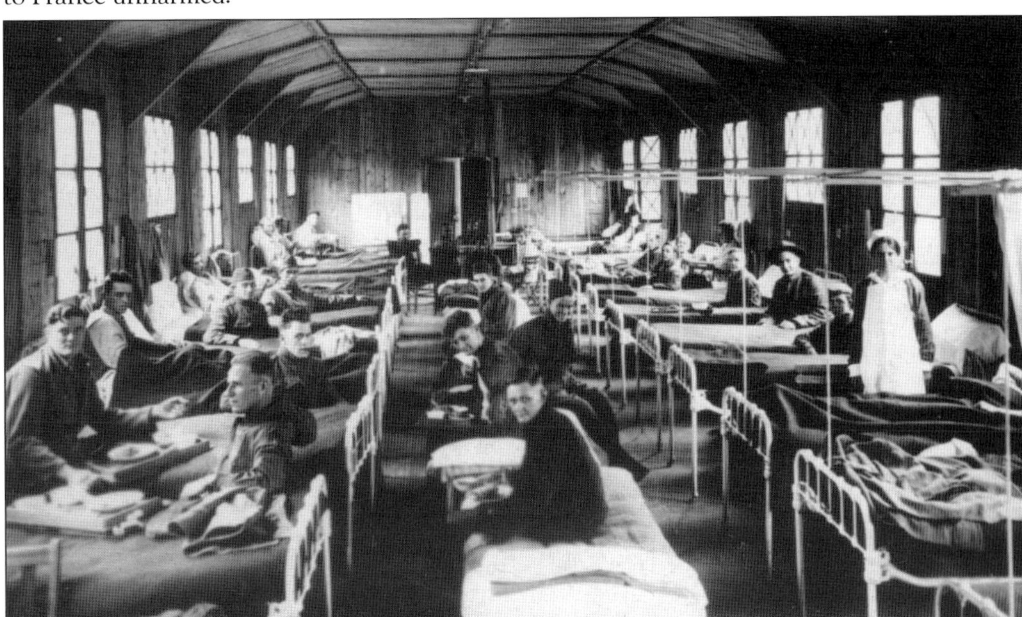

The Harper unit was stationed at Base Hospital No. 17 in Dijon, France, where the nurses would spend the remainder of the war tending to the wounded from the western front. The hospital was run out of a main building and a series of individual huts dedicated to a medical treatment. This is an interior view of the Gassed Patients Ward. Ms. Hellgrew, a Harper nurse, stands on the right. The black tape on the windows was placed to reinforce against air raids.

The 36th Base Hospital was organized out of the Detroit College of Medicine on April 11, 1917. It consisted of 24 officers, 100 nurses organized under the auspices of the Red Cross, and 200 enlisted men. The men drilled two to three nights a week, mostly at Eastern Market or Belle Isle. The unit mobilized on August 23, 1917, and encamped at the state fairgrounds for several months before being called to war.

In the fall of 1917, the unit was sent to France and was the first hospital unit of over 1,000 beds to be deployed overseas. The hospital was based out of Vittel, France, in a series of five hotels, a villa, and smaller outbuildings. Because the hotels were located at a distance from each other, they took on the names A, B, C, D, and E, and each had their own specialty. Under the direction of Maj. Burt Shurly, the staff treated approximately 15,000 casualties during the war. This is a view of Hospital B, home of Surgical Services.

Four

INDUSTRY

World War I is often referred to as the first "modern war" because of the new technologies adopted for use, such as tanks, aircraft, machine guns, and the transition from horses to motor vehicles. This new kind of warfare demanded a dramatic expansion of industrial production, and no American city was as prepared to accept this challenge as Detroit.

As Detroit's community of industrial expertise was recognized by the government, many of its business leaders became involved in national affairs. Howard E. Coffin, "father of standardization" and founder of Hudson Motors, served on the Naval Consulting Board, created an inventory of the nation's industrial capacity, assisted in the development of the Liberty Engine, and served as chair of the Department of War Aircraft Board.

The draft emptied factories of experienced men. Their replacements, recruited straight from high schools and family homes, were new to industrial settings. Safety was a major concern, especially for employers of women, whose dresses were just as likely as their inexperience to cause an accident on the job. Voluminous dresses were often traded out for trim jumpsuits, and hair was covered with a cap if the nature of the work demanded it.

Chalmers Motor Company was one of the first to employ women in a variety of positions, including work on drill, bench, and milling machines, assembly and inspection work, and work in the foundry. The atmosphere was pleasant enough for a factory, and the ladies were given special restrooms where comfortable chairs, Victrola phonographs, and popular magazines were available during break. These photographs, taken in June 1917, show women working at different activities within munitions plants. Above, women work beside men to build large shell cores at the Aluminum Casting Company. Below, drill machine workers at Chalmers Motor Company practice their new trade.

The Morgan & Wright plant, located next to the Belle Isle Bridge, was one of the largest producers of tires in the country. Unlike many other area plants, Morgan & Wright did not have to retool to produce new products during the war years as government orders for ambulances and supply trucks meant that tires were in extremely high demand. Here, Morgan & Wright employees work tires by hand.

By May 1918, many companies involved in war production considered female workers the solution to labor shortages caused by the draft. Women were hired in relatively high numbers to perform jobs that did not require brute strength, and they quickly gained a reputation for excelling at detail work. Workers are pictured measuring and testing airplane parts in 1918. (NARA.)

The YWCA's War Work Campaign established Industrial War Service Centers throughout the United States to support the needs of women working in war industries. The centers were places where women could make friends, have access to a hot meal, relax, and participate in "wholesome" recreation. In this 1918 image, women gather around the piano at one of Detroit's Industrial War Service Centers to sing "The Sweet Long Ago."

Flush with war work, Maxwell Motors expanded its production capabilities by leasing an auto production plant on East Jefferson Avenue from Chalmers Motor Company. One of its new initiatives was to build an experimental model of the Class AA three-quarter-ton truck. Designed under the specifications of the Quartermaster Corps, Maxwell trucks were used by the Navy Department, the Marine Signal, and the Medical Corps. Here, workers are at welding stations at the East Jefferson plant in 1918.

The Maxwell Motors Oakland Avenue plant was retooled to produce munitions for the war effort. Seen here with a supply of 75-millimeter shells is 22-year old Myrtle Orr, who served as a quality-control inspector. Like many women, she chose to work in the munitions plant because she had a family member—her brother Jerome—who was fighting overseas, and she wanted to do her part to support the war effort.

Artillery tractors, which could haul supplies over uneven terrain, quickly replaced horses as the transportation method of choice. Maxwell Motors took on production for Holt Manufacturing when government orders exceeded its manufacturing capacity. Maxwell produced 2,193 of the five-ton armored vehicles during the war, several of which are seen here parked in the residential neighborhood outside of the Maxwell East Side factory.

Prior to 1917, American Car & Foundry was known primarily as a railcar-building company. During the war years, it produced a wide variety of products for the Allied forces, including ammunition, artillery gun mounts, field kitchens, and submarine chasers, as well as railcars. Munitions workers are seen here welding at their stations in the American Car & Foundry plant in Detroit in October 1918.

Early in the war, Secretary of the Navy Josephus Daniels (center) approached Henry Ford (left) to talk about the possible mass production of submarine chasers. Ford agreed to do so, and in January 1918 work began on the ships at the newly erected Building B at the Ford Rouge plant. This image was likely taken at the train depot in April 1918 during Daniels's visit to Detroit to check in on the progress of the ships.

Production of the 200-foot-long steel ships, known as Eagle Boats, was slower than expected, with only 7 of the 100 ordered by the Department of War completed on schedule. None made it to Europe by the Armistice. Here, five of the newly commissioned, waylaid crafts test their mettle in an unidentified body of water, most likely the Detroit River, in June 1919.

Though the Eagle Boat may have arrived too late to join the conflict, Ford Motor Company excelled in other areas of war production. Factories crafted Liberty Engines, petite M1918 tanks, steel helmets, submarine detectors, and lightweight plates for tanks, in addition to 6,000 ambulances and 33,000 cars. This is an exterior view of the Ford Motor Company Highland Park plant in 1917.

Ford's Model T was one of the most sought-after vehicles in World War I. The lightweight frame allowed for travel in areas that would bog down heavier vehicles, and the versatile chassis allowed it to transform into almost any kind of transport with help from aftermarket modifications. The chassis was used as the base for Allied forces' cargo trucks, troop transports, ambulances, and mobile command centers.

Some of the most influential machines that came out of Detroit during the Great War had little to do with munitions. German blockades and the horrific attrition rate of men and horses left Britain desperate to find a way to increase its food production capabilities. The Fordson tractor, produced at the Ford plant at Michigan Avenue and Brady Street, quickly became the hero of British farmers.

The Lincoln Motor Car Company, appropriately named for the patriotic sensibilities of the time, was founded in 1917 by automotive engineer Henry Leland and his son Wilfred C. Leland. Located at Warren and Livernois Avenues, the factory, a four-story building of cream-colored brick and limestone, was designed by Detroit architect George D. Mason and was completed within five months of ground-breaking. Its specialty was Liberty engines.

Besides manufacturing Liberty engines, Lincoln Motors ran a robust munitions program. Over 600 women were employed in the making of munitions, many who were war widows or had husbands in the service. Lincoln was the first war plant to engage women with oxyacetylene welding, a process demonstrated here in which the flame burns at about 3,500 degrees Celsius (6,330 degrees Fahrenheit).

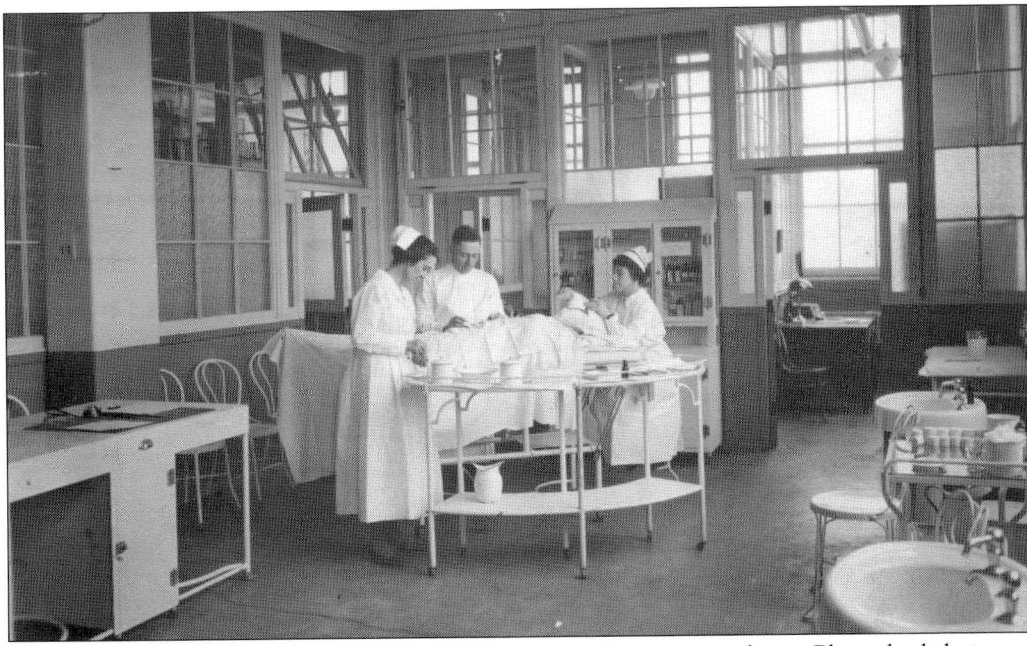

As government contracts increased, so did the scope of many war plants. Plants had their own sewer and water systems, roads, railroad links, fire departments, hospitals, cafeterias, and the occasional recreation facility. Most plants were fenced and guarded against possible sabotage or incursion. This is a view of the Lincoln Motors hospital staff in action in 1918.

Detroit longed to be the center for aviation manufacturing. Contracts for Liberty Aircraft production were given to five automobile makers by the Aircraft Production Board: Lincoln Motor Company, Packard Motor Car, Ford Motor Company, Nordyke & Marmon, and the Buick and Cadillac divisions of General Motors. Here, inspectors at Packard test Liberty engine parts in April 1918. (NARA.)

This is an exterior view of Fisher Body Corporation's Aeroplane Division in 1918. Between July 19, 1917, and December 24, 1918, the factory employed 4,500 workers and produced 400 JN1 training planes, 1,600 DeHavilland planes, four battle planes, and five Caproni bombers. After the war, Fisher Body was incorporated into General Motors, renamed the Fisher Fleetwood plant, and used to make Cadillac bodies. (Bentley.)

Fisher Body workmen carefully hand-stain and rub wooden propellers at the Aeroplane Division plant located on Detroit's West Side in 1918. At its peak, the plant employed 4,500 men and women and turned out an average of 40 planes per day. Fisher produced two kinds of aircraft for the war effort: the DH-4 and the Curtiss JN-4 "Jenny" trainer. (Bentley.)

During the war years, Packard's sprawling complex on East Grand Boulevard was one of the largest auto manufacturing plants in the United States. Packard turned to war work sooner than many other automobile companies and used its extra space to manufacture the Liberty V8 and V12 aero engines, as well as airplanes and other military transport. Packard employees are pictured assembling airplane fuselage and control parts. (National Archives.)

The Liberty engine manufacturer demanded precision in every step of the process, but many of the women and men hired to produce them had little background with industrial work. In response to this, vocational training was made available at most factories for employees who required it. Here, students study lengths and diameters during a class held in the Packard Motor Company machine shop around 1917 or 1918 (National Archives.)

Rigorous testing at multiple stages of the Liberty's life guaranteed that the standardized engine would perform as expected when called into action. At the Packard plant, engine testing took place in large sheds stationed outside of the main building. In these sheds, assembled engines would be tested, taken apart, and then reassembled. In this 1918 image, men work on the second assembly of engines. (National Archives.)

As one would expect, pride was apparent on the faces of Lincoln's executives when the 6,500th Liberty engine came through the line at the Lincoln Motor Company. Lincoln produced the largest number of engines of all the local contracts and consistently did so ahead of schedule. From left to right are Henry Leland, Charles Martens, W.H. Ebelhare, William Guy, P.W. Abbott, E.E. Sweet, W.C. Leland, W.T. Nash, and L.J. Williams.

Detroit's shipbuilding industry was utilized for war work prior to US intervention in 1917 by building craft for the United Kingdom and France. After 1917, most work went into building cargo ships for the US government. AmShip Detroit, formerly known as Detroit Shipbuilding Company, was the major manufacturer in the city, while Great Lakes Shipbuilding Company in Wyandotte, Michigan, dominated the scene downriver. Shown here is a view of the shipbuilding yards on Detroit's East Side.

On July 4, 1918, Great Lakes Shipping Company participated in a country-wide launch of newly built cargo ships. Three vessels—*Lake Janet*, *Lake Pearl*, and *Lake Silver*—were set to water. An employee-planned gala occurred after. The event included 15,000 people who listened to speeches delivered by the men who had built the ships and viewed a spectacular parade that included floats, banners, soldiers from Fort Wayne, and children representing the Boy Scouts and Campfire Girls.

The war industry was not the only place where women were employed in nontraditional roles. Detroit's women replaced clerks and postal workers and worked in transportation industries driving taxis and streetcars, manning railway crossings, and, as seen here, working the switches at railroad towers.

In response to a shortage of manpower, which was only expected to worsen once the latest draft selects were chosen, the Detroit Urban Railway (DUR) opened a school for training women in September 1918. The women attended Saturday classes, where lessons included how to operate doors, how to use the punch, make change, and read the signal system. A brief apprenticeship followed before the "conductorettes" took charge of a car of their own, typically on the Woodward Avenue line.

Five

CIVILIAN SUPPORT

The home front was just as important as the western front in the fight against the Central Powers. Civilians sacrificed and raised funds that sustained the war effort, powered the war industry, conserved food for the military and war relief, and volunteered with charitable organizations and campaigns. At a time when Detroit struggled to find its identity, the war mobilized the different elements of the city—social, ethnic, and economic—under a common cause.

Liberty Bonds were one of the most successful fundraising tools of World War I, bringing in a total of $18 billion during the 20-month-long conflict. The citizens and businesses of Detroit were enthusiastic supporters of the bond program and consistently surpassed their assigned quota of subscriptions. Shown here is one of the many promotional signs placed around the city during the third Liberty Loan campaign.

Detroit's collection of skyscrapers proved to be the perfect canvas for Liberty Loan and War Stamp advertisements. Here, the Real Estate Exchange Building wears a cartoon by Burt Thomas depicting an ailing Kaiser having his temperature taken with a thermometer. On the left side of the poster, men on scaffolding and in a harness repaint the sign to reflect recent progress made in Detroit's loan quota of $36 million.

The "Liberty Forum" was created in Campus Martius as a space where patriotic activities, such as Liberty Loan events, could take place. It consisted of speaker platforms, pillars, and various decorations. A separate "Liberty Way" ran along Woodward Avenue and featured countless feet of bunting, as well as statues of soldiers and the goddess Liberty. Here, crowds watch a sailor paint the backdrop of part of the forum. (Bentley.)

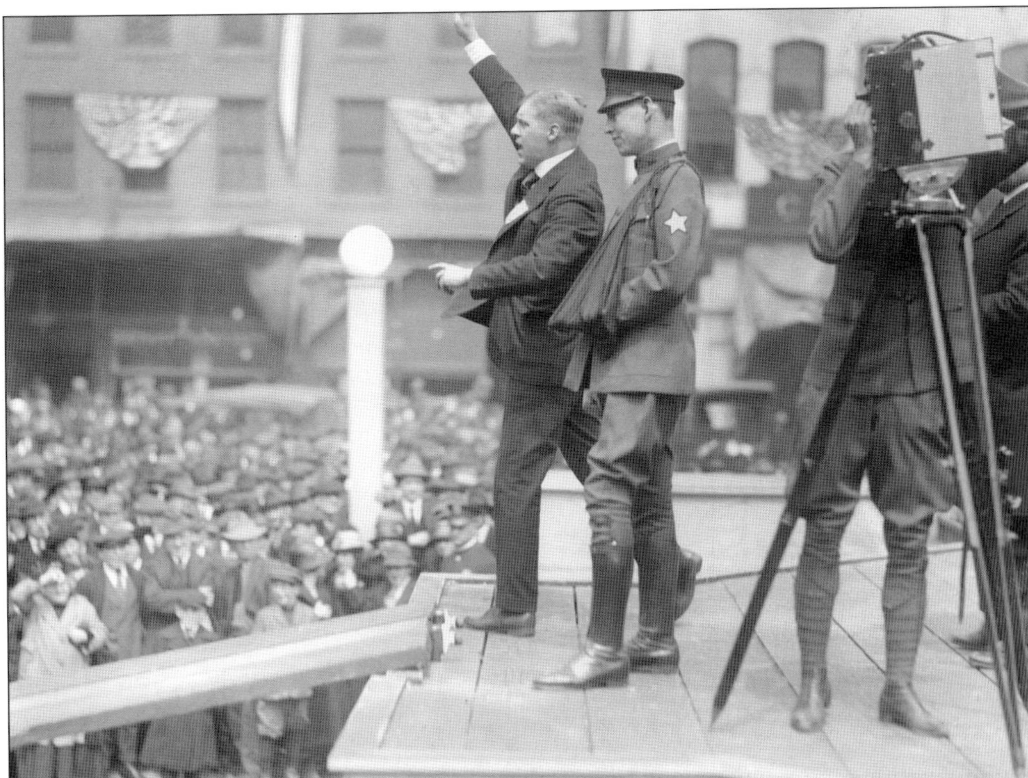

Liberty Loan rallies aimed to draw the maximum number of people, typically doing so by tempting the populace with musical performances, parades, and guest speakers. Politicians of local and international standing, military officers and heroes, orators, and members of the community all came to speak, though it was the artists and entertainers who felt most at home in front of the large crowds. Here, James Frederick Lawton, the beloved southeast Michigan poet and composer, engages the audience at a Liberty Loan drive.

Canadian actress Marie Dressler, best known for her comedic roles in vaudeville and early film, spent much of 1918 in roles that supported the Allied war effort. Besides performing for members of the American Expeditionary Forces, she toured the nation selling Liberty Bonds. Dressler speaks to Detroit's adoring crowds in this image.

The crowds were massive in downtown Detroit during a rally in support of the fourth Liberty Loan. In the background, a large replica of the Statue of Liberty stands with a plaque that reads: "They Died for Liberty." The statue was on a tour of select cities; however, Detroit loved her so much that the city bought her outright with the hope that she would serve as a permanent war memorial.

War plants were popular places to recruit for Liberty Loans, because the money raised during Detroit drives would ultimately come back to the city in the form of government contracts. War plants and their employees were generous, likely from an equal mixture of self-preservation and patriotism. Dodge Motor Company and its employees took on $1.5 million in Liberty Loans during the first drive alone. Here, an indoor war bond rally is being held at a Dodge manufacturing plant. (Burton.)

Parades were a popular form of entertainment and support, with turnouts ranging from dozens to hundreds of thousands. Outside of the Armistice celebration, Detroit's largest parade was held for the Detroit Patriotic Fund in May 1918. An estimated audience of 200,000 was in attendance. The parade was a marvel of color, design, and planning. Many of the floats and costumes were designed by Sam Hume of the Arts and Crafts Theatre. Seen here is Mrs. Francis Clark, the goddess atop the "Charity" float.

Of the many floats that sailed down Woodward Avenue, perhaps the most spectacular showing was by the "Spirit of the Red Cross" float and its retinue. The ship carried the children of men serving overseas and featured "the Sister of Mercy" flanked by two Knights Templar. Outriders from the Grosse Pointe Riding and Hunt Club carried the colors, and hundreds of Red Cross volunteers marching behind the float.

The Detroit Recreation Department sponsored parades in support of the war effort throughout 1917 and 1918. Shown here are children carrying farming tools and produce grown from war gardens. A banner reads: "Food will win the war—don't waste it!" A child pushes a wheelbarrow of homegrown bounty with signs stapled to its side supporting the purchase of government bonds. Smaller shows of community support such as this were common occurrences during Liberty Bond drives.

Members of the Detroit Liberty Band pose for a photograph in the spring of 1918. The 100-piece band was made entirely of volunteer musicians. Its leader, Lieutenant Dickerson, is seen standing at right. The band played during Liberty Loan events, fundraisers for charities, and parades for returning troops.

Hugh Chalmers, chairman of the Red Cross Campaign, addresses the audience in front of city hall during the Melting Pot Meeting in June 1917. The fundraiser brought in $2.5 million for the organization and featured two Detroit representatives from each of the Allied countries. The themes of the melting pot and Americanization were widespread during the war as the city tried to join its various elements—including social class and ethnic background—into one united support system.

Miss Detroit, aka Mrs. Homer Johnson, is seen here dropping the first gold coin into a flag to mark the beginning of Detroit's "Fill the Flag" campaign, sponsored by the Detroit Patriotic Fund. The campaign aimed to raise $7 million in seven days. The weeklong event culminated in a massive parade of 25,000 marchers from various Detroit charities. Flanking Miss Detroit are members of the Great Lakes Naval Band and a Boy Scout.

The pressure to support the Liberty Loans campaign was immense, yet the $50 bonds were out of reach for many. In an effort to reach a wider audience of patriots, the government created War Savings Stamps. The stamps came in two varieties: a 25¢ Thrift Stamp and a $5 War Savings Certificate. Mayor Oscar Marx is seen here buying Detroit's first War Savings Stamps from a cart positioned outside of Detroit City Hall on May 1, 1918.

By the end of the first year, Detroit had given 45,000 of its men to the armed forces and raised over $200 million through Liberty Loans, donation, and taxes—an average of about $200 for each man, woman, and child in the city. Seen here are munitions workers wearing sashes that encourage men to join the Navy march down Woodward Avenue during a fundraising parade in April 1918.

One of the more popular civilian activities during the war was the sewing and knitting campaign. Patterns for socks, scarves, vests, and hats were made available to the public, which took up needles in earnest. Scrap fabric and donated clothing was reworked into pretty frocks for war orphans and fur-lined vests for aviators. This display assembled by the women of the St. Clair branch of the Daughters of the American Revolution shows a cheerful mannequin in uniform knitting. Each package contains a helmet, a sweater, and a pair of wristlets. (NARA.)

Although larger organizations like the DAR (pictured) and Red Cross produced most of the work, smaller groups like the Boy Scouts and Campfire Girls and individuals ranging from firefighters to schoolchildren made thousands of garments for men in service. Knitting bags became fashionable accessories with women from all classes, and yarn shortages were not uncommon due to conservation efforts and the zeal of the volunteers. (NARA.)

A soldier holds American and British flags aloft in a symbol of solidarity as Detroit army recruits are treated to the hospitality of the Border Cities Welfare League of Windsor, Ontario. The women of the league provided cigarettes, writing materials, and other small comforts to American servicemen who passed through their city en route to Europe.

Individuals and small aid organizations, particularly those based in immigrant communities, played a large role in securing funds for war relief. An estimated $15 million was collected on behalf of servicemen and former countrymen in Europe and Asia Minor by these organizations, with significant representation from Detroit's Belgian, Jewish, Russian, Armenian, Serbian, Polish, Greek, and Italian communities. Here, Belgian refugees, including evacuated orphans, parade on Woodward Avenue in July 1917.

Detroit industrialist David A. Brown was a legend in the philanthropic community. During the years surrounding the war, Brown mobilized Detroit's Jewish community as general director of the Campaign for the Relief of Jewish Victims of the War and national chairman of the Jewish Joint Distribution Committee. On a secular level, Brown served in leadership positions with the United War Work Campaign, the Detroit Community Campaign, and the Red Cross.

"Give more than your share" was the motto for the Campaign for the Relief of Jewish Victims of the War, and Detroit's Jewish community rallied to the call of war relief from the early years of the conflict. Its contributions to charitable campaigns—both national Jewish aid efforts and local drives—are remarkable considering the majority of the 25,000 Jewish residents were immigrants with limited resources. Women's groups from Temple Beth El and Shaarey Zadek formed Red Cross units. Volunteers from the Jewish Student's Society canvassed neighborhoods in fundraising drives and held informational meetings at the Jewish Institute on High Street. Houses of worship, like the spectacular Temple Beth El on Woodward Avenue seen below, were anchors of community organization in relief efforts. At left is a poster sponsored by the Jewish Relief Campaign featuring a woman, presumably representing America, offering food to starving European woman and children. (LOC.)

United War Work Campaign was an interfaith effort between seven of the major charity organizations working in the United States to streamline fundraising and distribution of resources. Participants included the American Library Association, YMCA, YWCA, National Catholic War Council, Knights of Columbus, Jewish Welfare Board, Salvation Army, and War Camp Community Service. This is a fundraising board of a local branch of the Knights of Columbus around 1917 or 1918. (Burton.)

The Jewish Welfare Board saw to the spiritual needs of Jewish men in the military. It maintained chapels in military facilities, recruited and trained rabbis for military service, ensured that kosher food was available in canteens and barracks, and sponsored social activities such as dances, classes, and literary clubs. Jewish servicemen are observing Seder en route to Detroit from the western front in April 1919. (College of Charleston.)

The Red Cross was the grand lady of all of the volunteer organizations. It had the broadest reach in its mission, both socially and economically, and the widest range of volunteers. Though most leadership positions were filled by prominent women in society, the majority of the volunteers came from backgrounds that ran the social gamut. Poor women, middle-class women, immigrant women, and women of different races and faiths all played vital roles. Through different departments, the Detroit Red Cross volunteers served as nurses at home and abroad, assisted in the rebuilding of Europe at the conclusion of the war, made surgical dressings and bandages, made clothing for soldiers and war orphans, served as ambulance drivers and stretcher bearers for local hospitals, engaged in social work with veterans and their families, worked in food conservation, fed soldiers, and put in countless hours of fundraising.

Most of the train stations in the major cities across the United States had a Red Cross canteen. Michigan Central Station housed the city's canteens in the basement of the station and in a railcar in the Wabash yard during both of the World Wars. The canteens served 18,000 soldiers weekly. Red Cross volunteers plied weary travelers with coffee, baked goods, and fresh fruit during the brief stop in their travels.

The work of the 280 canteen volunteers was one of quiet hours and sudden bursts of excitement. Much time went into the preparation of food: endless peeling, chopping, and mixing. Soldiers fortunate enough to have a layover between trains were treated to a full meal in the basement canteen. For those who did not have time to disembark, the canteen workers provided coffee and sandwiches through the railcar windows. (NARA.)

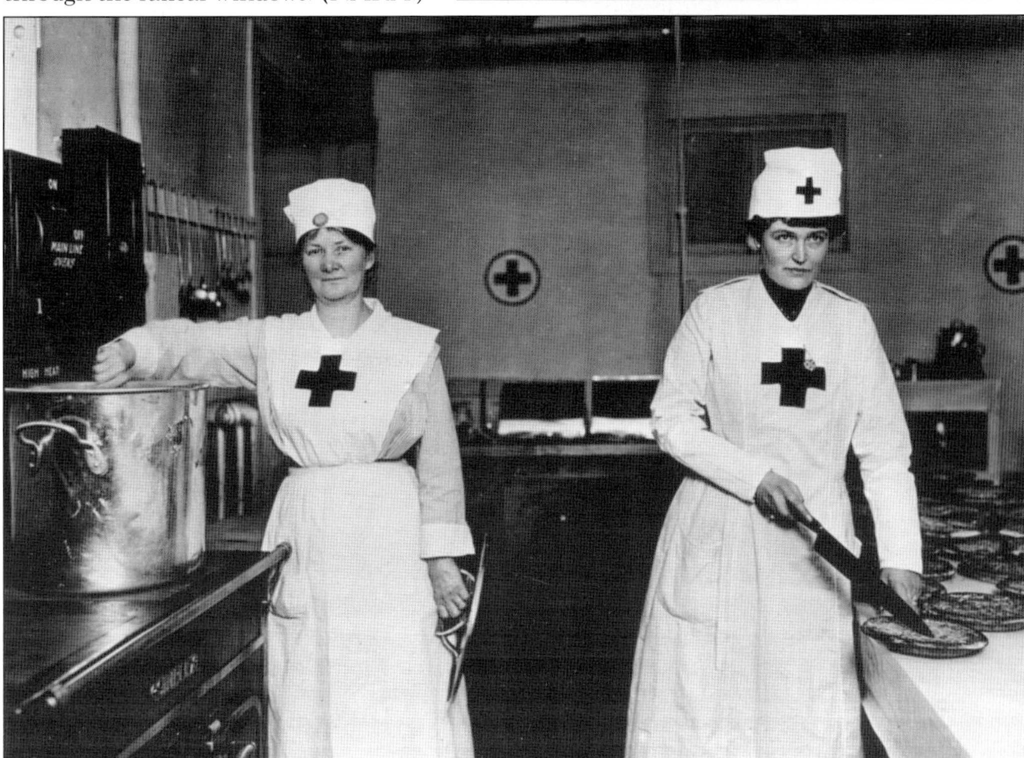

While private fraternal organizations often worked out of established homes, volunteer organizations, such as the Red Cross, typically made due with borrowed space from public or private buildings. Libraries and schools were the most common home to Red Cross units. This is a photograph of the Red Cross unit of the Utley Library branch, taken in March 1918, as volunteers make surgical dressings for field hospitals.

Members of the Junior Red Cross (JRC) knitted clothing, rolled bandages, tended war gardens, rehabilitated used materials, fundraised, sent letters to soldiers, and made "friendship boxes" for needy children overseas. Locally, Detroit had approximately 100,000 members. In this photograph, members of the JRC at Morley Elementary School celebrate reaching "100%" (enrolling 100 percent of their school in the JRC) with a parade through the neighborhood.

Throughout the war, the Detroit Red Cross sponsored a "Wealth from Waste" campaign, which gathered unwanted material, repaired it, and sold it at auction or through a storefront. The funds raised were used to support their war services. A huge crowd has filled the street in front of Family Theatre as a man auctions off tires in July 1918. US Marines signs line the platform.

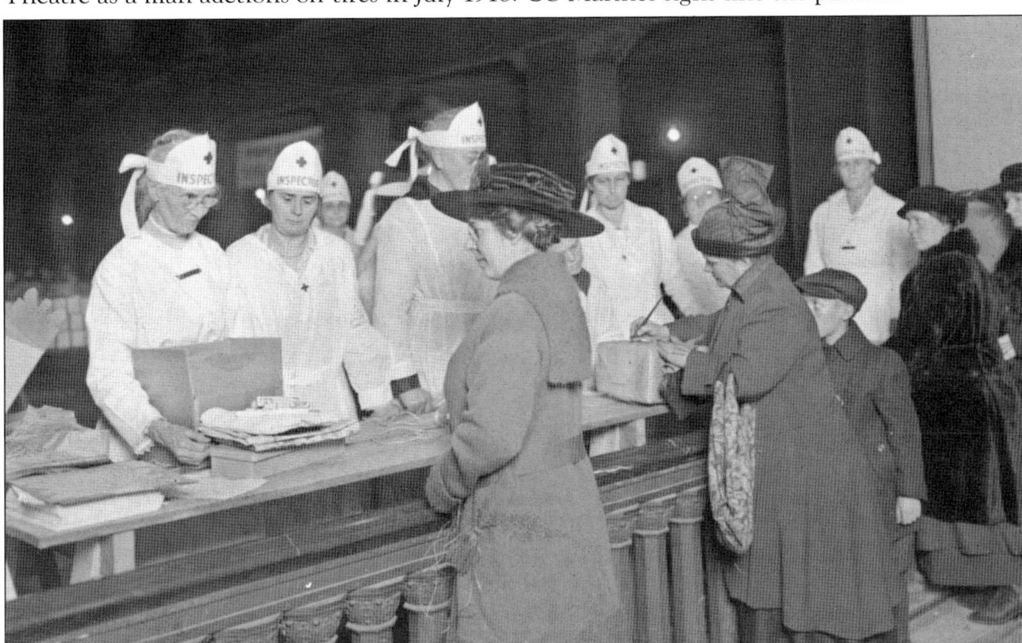

Red Cross postal inspectors worked tirelessly through October and November of each year to ensure that Christmas packages followed federal guidelines. Special labels were required to send material overseas and came directly to families from soldiers. Servicemen without family in the city sent their labels to the post office, where people could sign up to make a box for the "orphans."

Red Cross Parades were large, impressive affairs that served as fundraisers to support the organization's work. The Red Cross sponsored several parades during the war, and its members could be counted on to participate in any parade or public celebration of the war effort. A Red Cross volunteer guides a bandaged soldier down Woodward Avenue during a parade in 1917 or 1918. In the background, a Boy Scout follows with a wheelchair.

Smaller fraternal and social organizations played an important role in the war effort. The Order of the Eastern Star, some of whose members are seen here, were busy throughout the war sponsoring activities on behalf of the American Fund for French Wounded and sewing garments, each containing a personal written message of cheer, for the Harper Hospital unit in France.

The National League of Women's Service (NLWS) was an organization created in 1917. In conjunction with the American Red Cross, it trained women to fill necessary jobs left vacant by enlisted men. Activities initially included motor driving and repair, medical training, map reading, and telegraphy, though as the war intensified, the scope quickly broadened to include the care and transport of wounded and convalescing soldiers. These volunteers are changing out damaged tires from a service vehicle.

Volunteers for the NLWS were called primarily from the "comfortable classes," as each woman needed to have her own vehicle. These members of the Motor Division are learning how to navigate the workings of the automobile motor during a class at Cass Technical High School in July 1918. The purpose of the course was to familiarize women with engine repair so that they might serve as ambulance drivers at home or abroad. Over 50 Detroit NLWS volunteers served in France.

The War Camp Community Service was established to act as a clearinghouse for information pertinent to enlisted men and to organize recreation activities for soldiers and sailors in areas adjacent to military bases or otherwise affected by military presence. In Detroit, the service hut was in the heart of it all on Campus Martius.

The War Camp Community Service hut was useful for sharing information, but it lacked some of the creature comforts of home. The WCCS established an Army & Navy Club at Madison Avenue and Grand Circus to provide American and Canadian enlisted men with wholesome recreation opportunities and a place to have a hot, home-cooked meal. Soldiers and sailors are seen tucking into lunch in the Army & Navy Club's basement canteen.

In the spring of 1918, the YMCA set up a "Y" hut on Elizabeth Street, the first of its kind in the United States. "Y" huts were used throughout Europe as rest and recreation spaces for soldiers. The hut featured an auditorium that could be turned into a dormitory, a lounge, locker room, showers, office, and kitchen. (Bentley.)

The YWCA provided support services to women affected by the war. Locally, they sponsored centers for war workers and provided assistance to military families. At Camp Custer, they built a Hostess House to facilitate family visits. Abroad, they supported thousands of women workers and volunteers and assisted with the postwar reconstruction. Volunteers from the Detroit Metro YWCA inspect the shell-battered remains of their former building in Varennes, France. (Bentley.)

On June 19, 1918, the city came out to see its first glimpse of a tank, the famed *Britannia*, star of the Battle of Arras. *Britannia*, seen here outside of Campus Martius, toured the United States in patriotic fundraising campaigns. In Detroit, she was used to raise money for War Savings Stamps ($10 in stamps guaranteed a ride) and as a tool for the British-Canadian recruiting mission.

In July 1918, Detroit was wild with excitement over a visit from the legendary Chasseurs Alpins, an elite regiment of mountain infantrymen from the French Army. The unit gained the nickname "Blue Devils" from its fierce fighting record, evidenced here by the numbers of medals decorated on each man. The majority of the representatives from the unit were brought onto the North American publicity tour so that they could recover from wounds while still serving the war effort.

On August 21, 1918, twelve planes from the American Flying Circus flew in a mock air battle at the Warren Avenue field. Led by special guest Brig. Gen. Charles Lee of the British Royal Flying Corps, the exhibition was part of a nationwide tour to demonstrate the recent advancements in aviation and featured one local boy: Lt. John H. Stanley. Pictured are members of the AFC tending to the fastest of the circus's planes.

A theme of patriotism permeated the activities of the children during the 1918–1919 school year. Classes started a week early with the expectation that most children would miss a week of school during the fourth Liberty Loan campaign. Less lighthearted was the elimination of German language courses from the curriculum in favor of a course in patriotism. These children from the Johnson Elementary School sit in a classroom decorated with patriotic flair. (Burton.)

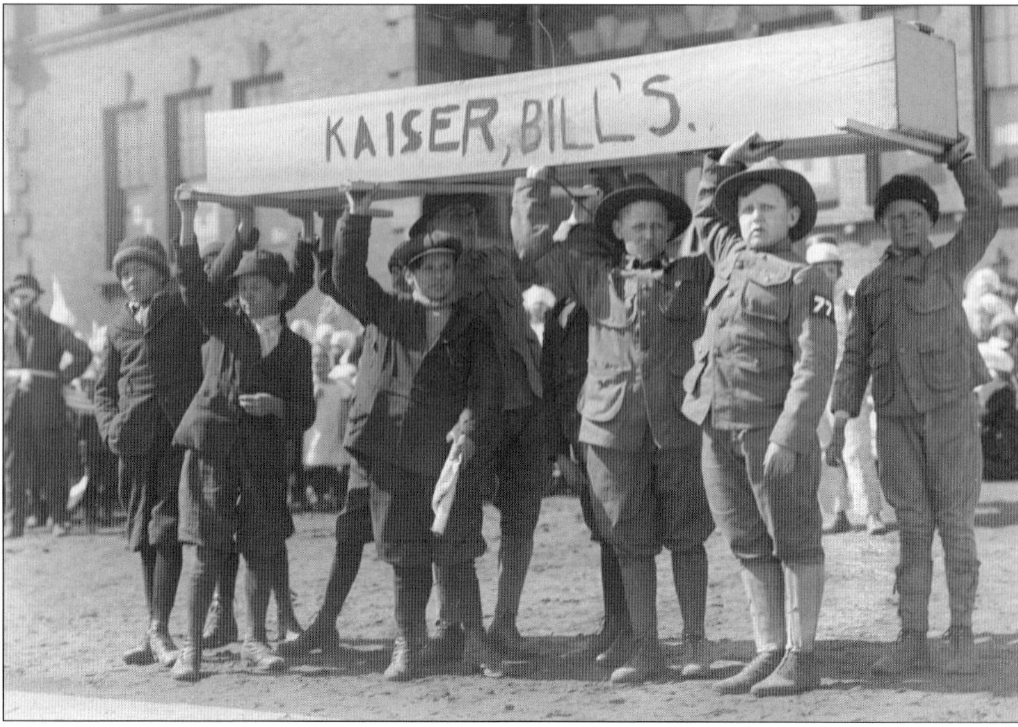

The Boys Scouts of America were a relatively new organization when America entered the war, but they wasted no time getting involved. Scouts, typically working with the Junior Red Cross, knitted for soldiers, made toys for orphans, tended war gardens, and participated in fundraising for charities. Notably, they played a vital role in the success of the War Stamps and Thrift Stamps campaigns, going door-to-door soliciting commitments. Above are the lads from Troop 77 holding a coffin for the Kaiser during a Red Cross parade. Below, other children elicit laughs from the crowd at the same event as they lead along a small, rather unimpressed goat who carries a sign that reads, "We have got the Kaiser's Goat," a joke based on popular a song of the same name.

America did not have mandatory rationing during World War I, but a general call went out for people to conserve items in high demand by the military, such as red meat, wheat flour, and sugar. "Meatless Tuesdays" were practiced in many Detroit homes as well as all hotels, and a conservation kitchen was set up on lower Woodward Avenue to teach people how to cook with wartime substitutes. Here, the windows of Shreve Grocery serve as a display for conservation posters. (NARA.)

Another fine example of conservation promotion is the large billboard seen here looming over Woodward Avenue on the J.L. Hudson and Co. Department Store. The text reads, "We Must Save Food over Here to Gain Victory over There." Throughout the war, Hudson's also donated space in its front windows for displays by organizations such as the US Food Administration, the DAR, and the Red Cross. (NARA.)

Wax statues of Pres. Woodrow Wilson made the rounds throughout the country in January 1918 to promote the War Savings Stamps drive. Statues were placed in display windows of department stores with patriotic bunting and signage. The statues were also used to endorse other war activities, such as food conservation and Liberty Loans. Detroit's Wilson doppelganger resided at the Emporium Department Store at Gratiot and Library Avenues. (NARA.)

War Gardens, also called Victory Gardens, were popular ways for people to contribute to the food conservation effort by providing themselves with fresh produce. The gardens dotted parcels of land throughout the city in over 100 empty lots and public spaces, all of which was condoned by Mayor Marx. Children at the Kirby Street garden, located at Kirby and John R. Streets, tend their garden on a sunny morning in July 1917.

In spring 1918, a model Victory Garden was established on the front lawn of the downtown library at Gratiot Avenue and Farmer Street. The garden was used as an educational tool to help inform the public on best gardening practices and food conservation topics like canning and preserving. A library assistant was on hand "every fine day" at a stand in the garden to check out books and distribute seed catalogs and government pamphlets.

For many, the cost rather than conservation of food was of primary concern. Prices rose steadily during the war, and by the summer of 1918, Detroit ranked 10th in the nation for high food prices. Lively Eastern Market was the shopping destination for wholesale vendors, grocery stores, and residents of the lower East Side. It became a popular destination with upper- and middle-class families looking to save money on their grocery bills, as well as a supplier of food for local military spaces, such as Selfridge Field.

Coal shortages plagued Detroit for much of 1917, with the issue coming to crisis during the particularly brutal winter of 1917–1918. In an effort to conserve coal, public recreation spaces, shops, and factories were all placed on reduced schedules. Only essential war plants were spared. Here, citizens line up outside of a coal yard armed with sleds and sacks, hoping to find fuel to bring home.

Family members of men in the service had few outlets of information to hear if their loved one had been injured, fallen ill, or killed. The most reliable was often the local newspapers, which published extensive casualty reports. The reports typically went into great detail, categorizing how the person died (i.e., illness, in action, etc.) or how severe their wounds were. Pictured are soldiers waiting with the bodies of the fallen at Michigan Central Station in 1918.

In the fall of 1918, the horror of Spanish Influenza arrived in Detroit. Despite the efforts of health commissioner David Inches (pictured), the disease spread quickly through the city. Schools and public venues (theaters, churches, etc.) were closed. Teachers were trained to serve as nurses and cared for invalids—approximately 102,000 house calls were made by educators at risk to their own health. By November 20, 1918, a total of 18,066 cases of influenza were reported in the city, with 1,688 fatalities.

Red Cross volunteers served as an auxiliary of the US Public Health Service during the influenza epidemic. Working shifts of 14 to 16 hours a day, nurses, Motor Corps, and canteen workers provided services impossible for the city to offer due to a lack of manpower. They nursed the sick, made home visits, transported victims to hospitals, and made food baskets and delivered them to people trapped in their homes by quarantine.

During the week of April 27 to May 4, 1918, the Women's Committee of the Council of National Defense held a nationwide registration of women to match individual skill sets with suitable war work or volunteer opportunities. In Detroit, registration booths were set up in public areas, such as clubs, theatres, and stores. The registered women showed a heavy interest in practical nursing and Red Cross work, though the city was keen to find replacement teachers for those lost to the war. The registration program was a success, with 10,000 women registered the first day. Seen here is "The Spirit of Woman-Power," a striking publicity poster by Detroit artist Paul Honoré. (Grand Rapids Public Museum.)

Six

The War's End

Armistice was declared at Compiegne at 11:00 a.m. on November 11, 1918, marking the cessation of fighting between Germany and the Allied nations. With the war over, it was time to see how Detroit would come to terms with the social, physical, and economic changes of the past 18 months. But heavy questions could wait; the city had a party to attend, a party the likes of which would probably never be seen again.

The horns and church bells started before daybreak, sounding the end of the war. Thousands of revelers rose quickly and descended upon the area surrounding the Liberty Forum, where speeches were delivered in English, Italian, and Greek. A holiday was declared, and schools, factories, and shops were closed to allow the city to celebrate together. Here, the sun rises over early morning crowds at Campus Martius.

The din raised by the crowd was terrific. Spontaneous group song permeated the day, and elated celebrants sounded horns, pots and pans, and musical instruments in the streets. These merrymakers carried flags of Allied nations as they serenaded downtown Detroit.

There were bonfires, music, and dancing in the streets in the neighborhoods, but eventually it seemed that most people found their way downtown for the main event. The gray November morning was alive with the colors of thousands of waving flags and storms of confetti.

Happy chaos reigned in the streets that day. Among the many banners, flags, and decorated cars that weaved through the celebration, effigies of the Kaiser were among the more popular accessories of the event. The cartoonish sack dolls were lighthearted for the most part, though most would not make it through the day intact.

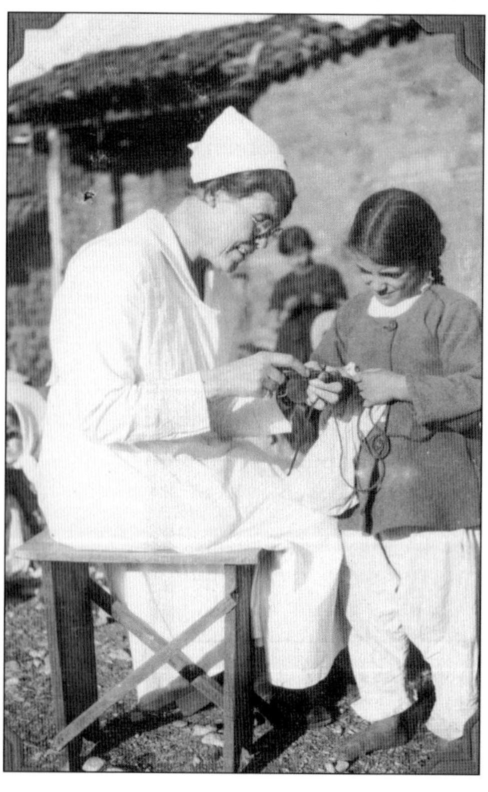

Victory celebrations quickly spread from the streets into businesses throughout the city. Factories that supplied the war industry were especially jubilant, often staging elaborate pageants to honor the hard won Allied victory made possible through their own labor. This is a scene staged by employees of the Lincoln Motor Company.

Though the war ended in 1918, many women who served overseas remained in Europe to assist with the aftermath. Johanna Eriksson, a Detroit nurse attached to Base Hospital No. 17, stayed behind for several years as part of the American Red Cross. Her experiences working with orphans and public health initiatives in Eastern Europe are documented in a scrapbook held at the Reuther Library. In this 1919 image, Eriksson teaches a young Albanian girl how to knit.

Michigan men started trickling into the country beginning in December, although the "Michigan majority" units would not arrive until spring. For the Detroit men serving in out-of-state units, the trip home started in New York City, where ships like the *Mauretania* would transfer them via ferries and trains to Army camps. The welcome in New York was mighty, as troopships were greeted by the cheers of crowds and whistles from ships that flanked them in the harbor with flags waving. The men would have their belongings fumigated and washed, get deloused, and then have a medical examination before they were sent off with a month's pay and a train ticket home.

The French hospitals started transferring casualties home en masse during this time. The Department of War sent men to hospitals within 300 miles of their nearest relatives, which for Detroit's men meant General Hospital No. 36 (Ford Hospital) or the base hospital at Camp Custer. Here, John Zeldham (in wheelchair) receives a citation while convalescing at Camp Custer on February 24, 1919. (Bentley.)

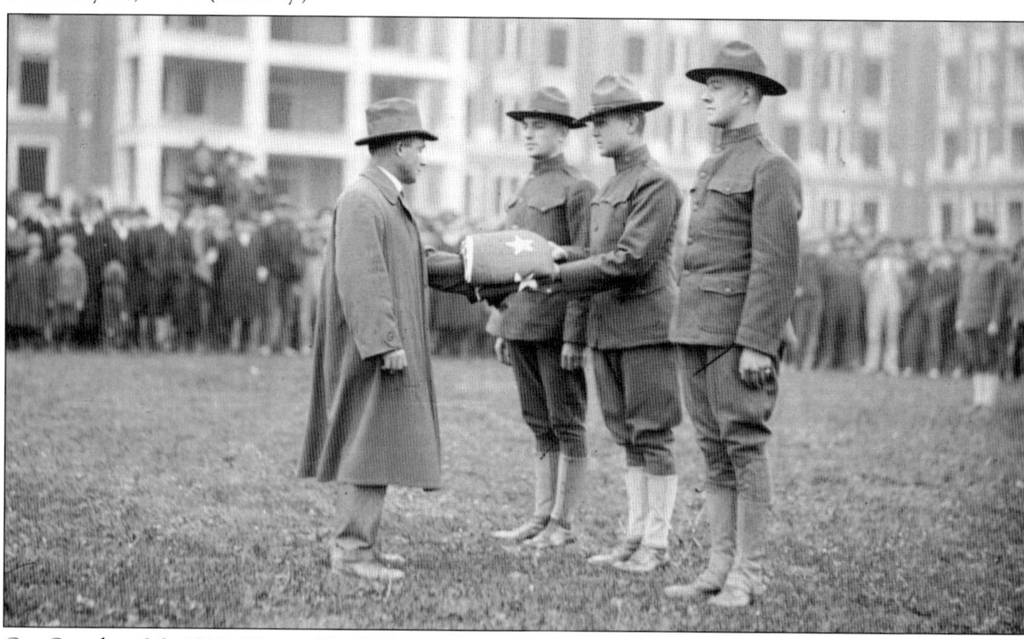

On October 26, 1918, Henry Ford Hospital was transferred to the US Army, which renamed it US General Hospital No. 36. Though the hospital was not yet fully constructed, it played an important role in the lives of Detroit's servicemen. Completed portions of the building were used to provide much needed medical service and therapy for approximately 2,000 wounded veterans as they returned from overseas.

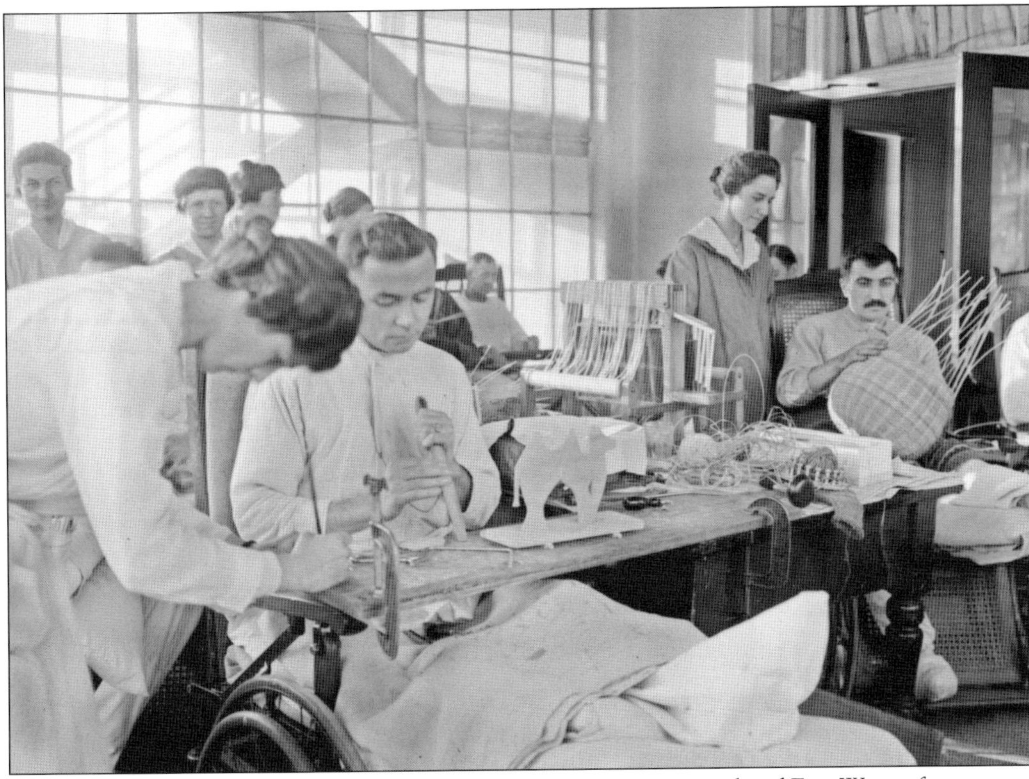

The Red Cross ran occupational therapy classes out of Harper Hospital and Fort Wayne for returned wounded soldiers. The men participated in activities that would "keep them busy" while they convalesced. In the case of men who had lost or damaged limbs, the projects helped them fine tune their motor skills while working with only one arm or limited vision. Pictured are soldiers and their teachers at Harper Hospital passing an afternoon crafting.

Approximately 175,000 Michigan men served in the armed forces during World War I. Nearly 70,000 of the men were from Detroit. During the conflict, 485 of the men died from injury or disease and countless others sustained grievous wounds. This military funeral occurred in September 1918.

Throughout the spring, the troops came home, almost always to a grand celebration. Parades and public ceremonies were common, and huge crowds would come out to show appreciation to the soldiers and their sacrifices. Seen here are members of the 32nd Division as they come under friendly fire from women armed with handfuls of confetti during their homecoming celebration in May 1919.

The 16th Engineers made a brief appearance in Detroit upon their return stateside on May 12, 1919. Led by Col. Harry Burgess, they marched from Michigan Central Station down Michigan Avenue to Woodward Avenue, then to Grand Circus Park, and then finally looped back to the station. The men re-entrained to Camp Custer, where they were mustered out into civilian life.

Prior to boarding the train at Michigan Central Station, the regiment was presented with a commemorative silk flag. William Livingstone, father of Capt. Palmer Livingstone, served as the flag bearer. Mrs. R.H. Strohmer, mother of Master Engineer R.H. Strohmer Jr., is seen here presenting the flag to Colonel Burgess.

Cheers erupted as the first company of the 119th Field Artillery swung out of Michigan Central Station upon its return home on May 12, 1919. The Guardsmen marched towards downtown, surrounded by thousands of well-wishers. Their destination was the armory, where they would be reunited with family members for a few hours before re-entraining to Lansing for a celebration at the capitol.

The celebration was unforgettable with the 119th Field Artillery Band leading the march out of the station. The band members were temporarily impeded from playing by mothers and sweethearts who rushed the column to hold onto their arms. The Liberty Band followed, playing "The Victors" as hundreds of high school boys chanted in appreciation. The crowds filled in the rear as the parade passed, flooding the streets curb to curb, with the merry group making its way down Woodward Avenue toward the armory.

Officers from the 125th Infantry Brigade of the 32nd Division pose for a photograph outside of railcar, presumably in New York, upon their return to the United States on May 12, 1919. From left to right are Lieutenant Niblock; Capt. E.M. Connor; Capt. Edward Heckel; Lt. Col. Milton Hinkey, recipient of the Croix de Guerre; and Capt. Frank H. Mis.

Children holding American flags line up on a curb to celebrate the return of the "Red Arrows" from the western front. The Michigan units of the Red Arrow Division (32nd Infantry Division) included the 125th and 126th Infantry Brigades and the 120th Machine Gun Battalion. The three groups arrived home to Detroit on May 18, 1919. The next day was declared a holiday, with all schools, government offices, and businesses closed to celebrate "Red Arrow Day."

The Red Arrow Division gained its name from its service in France, where it pierced enemy lines "like a red arrow." The division was known for its fierceness in battle and fought in three major offensives: the Aisne-Marne, Oise-Aisne, and Meuse-Argonne. The Red arrows met and defeated 23 German divisions, repulsed every counter attack, and captured over 2,100 prisoners. Here, members of the Red Arrow Division march triumphantly down "Victory Way" on Woodward Avenue during their homecoming parade.

The 125th Infantry Brigade was created from parts of the 31st and 33rd National Guard Regiments. Its men were the first Americans to fight on German soil. For that honor, their casualty rate was extreme: 125 officers and 3,151 men. To put that in perspective, their original maximum "war strength" was 3,200; thus, they had a casualty rate over 100 percent. Here, exuberant relief and pride emits from the crowd as they see the men safely back home.

Red Arrow Day was filled with parades, ceremonies, and dancing. Each soldier was given a card with a "key to the city" in it. The card entitled the men to refreshments at stands throughout the city, free passage on a Belle Isle ferry, entry to any theater or Navin Field, and entrance to a dance on Washington Boulevard. Pictured are soldiers happily marching through streets decorated in their honor.

One of the most remarkable stories to come from Detroit's units in World War I was that of the American North Russia Expeditionary Force (ANREF). ANREF was a contingent of men made mostly of the 339th Infantry Regiment, a battalion of the 310th Engineer Regiment, the 337th Ambulance Company, and the 337th Field Hospital. The units were broken off from the 85th Division upon their arrival in Europe in September of 1918 and sent to Archangel to protect stockpiles of Allied weapons and to fight against the Bolsheviks during the Russian Civil War. The group renamed itself the "Polar Bears" as a testament to the horrific conditions they endured throughout their nine-month assignment. The Polar Bears fought the Bolsheviks through the Northern Russian wilderness throughout the brutally cold arctic winter. Despite being weakened by disease, exposure, food shortages, and low morale, the Polar Bears managed many victories against enemy troops. Orders allowed the withdrawal of ANREF in April 1919, but the force stayed in Russia until early June because they were locked in by sea ice. Members of the 339th Infantry are pictured here on duty in Russia.

Dubbed locally by the press as "Detroit's Own" because of the large amount of Detroit men who served in it, the city took special pride in the Polar Bears. For months surrounding the Armistice, the soldiers' families, along with local editorialists and politicians, lobbied ferociously for their return to America. When the men arrived in the city on July 3, 1919, families and friends seemingly infiltrated every corner of Michigan Central Station. Above, friends and family members wait anxiously outside of the train station. Above them the banner reads, "Home at last! All Detroit welcomes home her 339th heroes." Below is a scene of happy chaos at Michigan Central Station as a Polar Bear happily returns to his mother's embrace.

A grand fête was planned in honor of the Polar Bears the next day, July 4, 1919. The men arrived on Belle Isle via the SS Britannia and were greeted by Red Cross workers bearing scented garlands of flowers. The island was dressed in her best for the celebration. Anything that could be decorated was decked in ribbons, flowers, and flags. In the background of this image is the exterior of the Belle Isle Casino covered in bunting and the flags of the Allied nations and the ANREF.

A full day was planned for the Polar Bears and their families. After the presentation of medals, there was swimming, parades, baseball games, picnics, and dancing on the green. Seven concerts provided music throughout the event, and the Detroit Yacht Club gave the men full privileges for the day. Men without families present were well taken care of by a fleet of volunteers.

In 1929, a recovery expedition, headed by five former Polar Bears under the auspices of the Veterans of Foreign Wars, set out to recover the remains of the Polar Bears buried in Russia. Service diaries were used to retrace the tracks of the unit through the Arctic, and 86 of the lost soldiers were recovered. On December 1, 1929, fifty-five caskets arrived in Detroit during, fittingly, an intense blizzard.

Large crowds braved the weather to view the cortege. After the coffins received state honors at Detroit City Hall, they were placed for public viewing for a week at White Chapel Cemetery in Troy, Michigan. Hundreds came out to White Chapel to pay their respects and join the families of the fallen in their sorrow.

The caskets were placed in vaults until Memorial Day 1919, when they were brought out for a military burial. The graves were placed surrounding a memorial statue of a white marble Polar Bear, created by French sculptor Leon Hermont. Here, Mr. and Mrs. Frank Skocelas hold the flag and are reunited with their son, Pvt. Andrew Skocelas, one final time.

Though troops were released from service gradually to prevent issues of unemployment, demobilization quickly flooded Detroit's job market with servicemen. In January, over 200 men were arriving back in the city every day. Many of them had to temporarily accept work in fields outside of their area of specialty until the market was able to adjust to postwar conditions. This is a view of a breadline in an unidentified Detroit neighborhood in 1919.

The majority of women employed as replacements for men, in heavy industry and otherwise, lost their jobs when veterans returned to the workforce; however, there were some exceptions. In January 1919, a ruling by the National War Labor Board determined that current female conductors on the DUR, along with 15 women who had just completed training, would remain on the job, though no additional women would be hired.

The war challenged many social norms regarding gender, with the greatest change being the shift in opinion on the issue of women's suffrage. The role women played in the war effort as volunteers, nurses, and war workers proved to many that women deserved a voice within the political realm. Suffrage passed in Michigan in November 1918, through strong support from military, industrial, and local political figures and by the tireless work of suffragettes.

The war continued to shape the face of the city years after its end. Europe's devastated economy made it nearly impossible for Slavic workers to return home, so many laid down permanent roots in Detroit. Thousands of Europeans looking to start fresh came to the city. Among the many groups who immigrated were the Maltese, who settled primarily around Corktown. Maltese factory workers are participating in an Americanization night school in 1920. (Bentley.)

The Veterans of Foreign Wars' "Daisy Drive" was a fundraiser that collected money for soldiers in financial need through the selling of fresh flowers. "Poppy Drives" were more commonly used by charitable organizations because the flower was linked with the World War I poem "In Flanders Fields." Regardless of the particular flora, flower drives were popular ways to show support for those who had served in the military, as well as those directly affected by the war, such as widows and orphans.

The first US soldier to perish on German-held land was a Michigan native, Joseph William Guyton of Evart. Guyton, a machine gunner for the 126th Infantry Regiment of the 32nd Division, was killed by enemy fire on May 24, 1918, in the Gildwilder Sector of Alsace. In 1921, the year Guyton's remains were returned to the United States, the Detroit Board of Education named a new school, located at 355 Philip Street, in his memory.

Of all of Detroit's memorials to the fallen soldiers of the Great War, perhaps the most beautiful (and functional) is the University of Detroit Memorial Clock Tower. Completed in 1926 on the McNichols Campus, the 175-foot-tall tower serves as both a memorial to the 12 University of Detroit men who lost their lives and as a chimney for the powerhouse.

World War Mother's of Detroit and Windsor came together on June 30, 1942, to dedicate a bronze tablet in memory of the sons lost in the Great War. The memorial tablet was placed on Belle Isle near the Peace Carillon. The dedication ceremony, seen here, was preceded by a parade from the Broadhead Naval Armory, which featured a presentation of colors and the Naval Armory Drum Corps.

Between 1919 and 1954, November 11 was a public holiday known as Armistice Day. The day was meant to be an opportunity to reflect on world peace and honor those who perished in "the war to end all wars." Veterans are seen marching down Woodward Avenue surrounded by cheering crowds during Detroit's 1938 parade, unaware that the next "Great War" was just on the horizon.